itsu

the cookbook

itsu

the cookbook

100 low-calorie eat beautiful recipes for health & happiness

Julian Metcalfe & Blanche Vaughan
Nutritional consultant Angela Dowden

MITCHELL BEAZLEY

itsu the cookbook

by Julian Metcalfe & Blanche Vaughan

First published in Great Britain in 2014 by Mitchell Beazley,
a division of Octopus Publishing Group Ltd, Endeavour House,
189 Shaftesbury Avenue, London WC2H 8JY
www.octopusbooks.co.uk

An Hachette UK Company
www.hachette.co.uk

Distributed in the US by Hachette Book Group USA,
237 Park Avenue, New York, NY 10017, USA

Distributed in Canada by Canadian Manda Group,
165 Dufferin Street, Toronto, Ontario, Canada M6K 3H6

Specially commissioned photography by Anders Schønnemann.

ISBN: 978 1 84533 898 5

Set in VAG Rounded LT.

Printed and bound in China.

Publisher: Alison Starling
Art Director: Jonathan Christie
Deputy Art Director: Yasia Williams-Leedham
Senior Editor: Leanne Bryan
Designer: Jaz Bahra
Illustrator: Abigail Read
Assistant Production Manager: Caroline Alberti

Copy Editor: Trish Burgess
Americanizer: Theresa Bebbington
Proofreaders: Jane Bamforth, Nicole Foster
Indexer: Isobel McLean
Photographer: Anders Schønnemann
Food Stylist: Annie Rigg
Assistant Food Stylist: Miranda Keyes
Nutritional Consultant: Angela Dowden
Props Stylists: Tabitha Hawkins and Jessica Georgiades

Notes:

Unless stated otherwise in the recipes:

- All calorie counts and fat content figures are per serving.
- All spoon and cup measures are level.
- All eggs are large.
- All vegetables should be peeled, as necessary.
- All herbs and leaves should be washed and trimmed, as necessary.
- Chiles can be used with or without seeds, depending on how spicy you like your food.
- Standard bunches of herbs in this book are ¾ ounce, small bunches are ⅓ ounce, and large bunches are 1 ounce. In comparison, a standard bunch of parsley or cilantro sold in U.S. supermarkets is 4 ounces.

This book contains some dishes made with raw or lightly cooked eggs. It is prudent for more vulnerable people, such as pregnant and nursing mothers, people with weakened immune systems, the elderly, babies, and young children, to avoid dishes made with uncooked or lightly cooked eggs.

Contents

Introduction

Like itsu, this book has been years in the making. We hope you find it inspirational and practical in equal measure!

The early pioneers of the British health-conscious, fast-food chain Pret A Manger are the creative force behind itsu. We opened our first award-winning restaurant on Brompton Cross, Chelsea, London in 1997. Years of listening and reacting to customers encouraged us to battle on and build a new type of food place dedicated to skinny but delicious food.

Over time, with untold hard work and passion, we morphed into an extremely busy, lighteningly fast takeaway place with thousands of discerning, loyal customers. We have managed to open another 50 itsu shops so far, many with loads of seats.

We still run our conveyor-belt restaurants with pride; we now call them itsu [dining] to distinguish them from our stores.

We have, almost by accident, become the world's first EAT BEAUTIFUL healthy fast-food bar … light, green, and good for you. Apparently, the secret to Pink Floyd's breathtaking music is as much about what they left out as what they put in, a bit like itsu: less fat, more bounce.

itsu pays homage to the remarkable cuisine of Japan, Korea, Vietnam, and Thailand—restaurant food, street food, chefs' food, home-cooked food—and many of the recipes that we serve in our stores and restaurants appear in this, our first cookbook. The recipes are light—all under 300 calories per person—and packed full of essential nutritional goodness.

Thank you to all our customers, inspiring management, and amazing staff for making itsu possible.

Endless gratitude to Blanche Vaughan, Celeste Tobias-Metcalfe, Pippi Brereton, William Da Silva, Tania Betley, and Nicola Formby for making this book a reality.

Julian Metcalfe

itsu orchids are fresh & beautiful
(a bit like our food...)

White orchids, in particular,
signify luxury & love.

The word orchid comes from
the Greek 'orkhis' meaning testicle...
on account of the shape of
its tuberous roots.

How to eat the itsu way

If you care about your body, you'll care about what you eat.
At itsu, we know that fabulous-tasting food can be good for you,
too, and the totally delicious recipes in this book prove our point.

Our formula is really simple: healthy + delicious = itsu. We take unprocessed raw ingredients that are naturally high in flavor while being low in saturated fat and calories (instead of artificially manipulated to be so), cook them simply and quickly, and serve them fresh.

The good news is that, even if you don't eat or cook the itsu way every day, you can still adopt the underlying principles and make significant changes to your health while keeping your taste buds happy, too. Here's how to incorporate some healthy eating into your life …

Embrace the Asian influence
The Japanese diet contains a lot of heart-healthy oily fish, plenty of high-protein, isoflavone-rich soy foods (some researchers believe that isoflavones help balance female hormones), and a smattering of iodine-packed seaweeds that can promote a healthy metabolic rate. So whether it's swapping a burger for a salmon steak, helping yourself to some nori-wrapped sushi for lunch, or popping some edamame (soybeans) into your salad, there are many ways you can and should incorporate an Asian theme in your diet.

A touch of *hara hachi bu*, which means "belly 80 percent full," is another Japanese habit that's well worth adopting. The idea is to stop eating before you're fit to burst, which can only be a good thing for your waistline and overall well-being.

Eat good fat
Having a healthy fat intake doesn't mean depriving yourself of every high-fat food, but it does mean moderating how much you consume and choosing the healthier types when you do indulge. This means that, while you might choose to eat less butter, cream, and red meat, you can enjoy healthy quantities of tasty nuts and seeds, oil-base dressings, avocados, and oily fish. By doing so, you'll be reducing your intake of saturated fat, which can contribute to clogged arteries, while making sure you get enough of the fats that are actively good for your heart. Plant and marine oils also provide the essential fatty acids that help nerve cells to communicate with each other and keep your skin healthy, thereby beautifying you from the inside out.

Moderate those carbs
When it comes to carbohydrates, it's good not to make them the focus of every meal (although current U.S. government advice says otherwise, which many consider outdated). But it's also good not to be completely carb-phobic (in an equally old-fashioned Atkins-esque kind of way). Instead, and in keeping with the itsu philosophy of food, the focus should be on having no more than fist-size portions of nutritious carbs, such as noodles, beans, pita bread, whole-wheat pasta, and brown rice. By doing this, and by avoiding too many high glycemic index (GI) foods, such as sugars and refined starches, which give you a quick energy boost followed by an equally rapid slump, you'll avoid constantly

flash-flooding your system with high levels of glucose and insulin. The happy result? You will decrease your risk of developing diabetes and heart disease, and find it easier to manage your weight.

Choose satisfying food

Managing your weight is all about feeling fuller on fewer calories and triggering the body's satiety signals, which is exactly what the recipes in this book achieve. Half the secret lies in eating mountains of crunchy and delicious vegetables, salads, and beans that score low on the energy-density scale (a fancy way of saying that they provide loads of stomach-filling bulk but few calories). The other half of the secret is in having a good helping of lean protein, such as chicken, shrimp, eggs, or edamame (soybeans), which we all tend to agree transform a less-than-filling snack into a proper meal. There's a good reason for this; protein has been scientifically proven to be the most satisfying nutrient. It's the perfect excuse for digging into some of your favorite foods.

Eat a rainbow

Fruit and vegetables in bright colors are particularly important sources of the antioxidants that can mop up cell-damaging free radicals. And those beautiful shades of orange, red, and purple are so gorgeously vibrant—one of the reasons many itsu dishes look so beautiful—that they'll cheer you up by just looking at them. In short, don't stop at just eating your greens; try to eat a rainbow of goodness, too.

Sprinkle some seedy goodness

You'll notice that many itsu recipes include a little sprinkle of superhealthy seeds. That's because they not only add some crunch but, from a nutritional perspective, they punch well above their meager weight. As a rule, seeds are good at making up the shortfall of valuable minerals that can sometimes be difficult to obtain in sufficient amounts from other sources. From the itsu pantry, just 1 tablespoon of sesame seeds provides around one-tenth of the recommended daily allowance (RDA) of magnesium, while 1 tablespoon of pumpkin seeds supplies a similar amount of the zinc RDA. Other great salad and soup sprinkles that can effortlessly increase your nutritional intake include finely chopped Brazil nuts (rich in selenium and magnesium), pine nuts (high in zinc), and hemp seeds (loaded with magnesium and iron).

And a little something of what you desire …

Last but not least, the itsu philosophy allows for some decadent treats. A little something of what you desire can only do you good. Using better ingredients with more intense flavors is the key to doing this well. For example, good-quality chocolate (containing 70 percent cocoa solids, as opposed to about 20 percent in ordinary milk chocolate) offers a more satisfying hit, so you can eat less while losing none of the enjoyment. Savor every mouthful, and remember that small can be beautiful.

Our recipes

If you've enjoyed eating at itsu when visiting the UK, this book now gives you 100 ways to re-create that dining experience in your own home. All the recipes within these pages—many of them itsu classics—are under 300 calories per serving, and the vast majority are low in saturated fat. Whether you're looking to feel more energetic, lose a few pounds (the recipes will fit neatly into a 5:2-style fasting plan), or just feel a little brighter and lighter, eating well has never been easier or tastier.

Glossary of terms & ingredients

Bonito flakes (*katsuobushi*): These are shavings made from dried, smoked fillets of bonito fish, which looks like tuna but is actually related to mackerel. Bonito flakes can be bought in airtight containers and are used for making *dashi*, or to sprinkle over food as a flavorsome seasoning.

Cellophane noodles: Made from rice, these dried noodles have a translucent quality, hence also being known as glass noodles. They come in various thicknesses, and our recipes use fine ones (resembling angel hair pasta) or flat ones (resembling tagliatelle).

Dashi: A Japanese stock made from *kombu* and *bonito flakes* that are steeped in boiled water. Dashi plays an important part in Japanese cooking and is used in a wide variety of dishes, including soups, sauces, dips, and omelet mixtures. You can make your own (*see* page 165), or buy instant dashi in packets from Japanese food stores or online.

Edamame: Small green soybeans bought in or out of the pod. They are available fresh or frozen from large supermarkets. High in protein, these beans can also help to regulate cholesterol levels.

Furikake: A Japanese seasoning made from black and white sesame seeds, ground *nori* and dried red *shiso* leaves. Delicious sprinkled over everything from rice to cooked fish or salads.

Ginger: Fresh or pickled, this warming spice has traditionally been used to boost circulation, ease joints, and aid digestion. In Japan, people like to eat pickled ginger between mouthfuls of sushi to cleanse the palate. Pickled ginger is available in larger supermarkets and online.

Glycemic Index (GI): A measure of how quickly a carbohydrate-containing food raises blood sugar levels. High GI carbs are rapidly broken down and assimilated, giving a big spike in sugar levels that may be followed by a slump; lower GI carbs are generally thought of as healthier because they give steadier sugar and energy levels and may fill you up for longer.

Japanese rice: *See* Sushi rice.

Kombu: A dried dark green seaweed that may be reconstituted in water. It is a good source of minerals, especially iodine, and adds *umami* flavoring to soups and stocks.

Maki: Rolled sushi (*see* pages 54–61).

Matcha: A powder made from ground green tea leaves; it is used in tea ceremonies or as a flavoring to make *mochi* (pounded sticky rice candies) and green tea ice cream.

Mirin: Low-alcohol sweet rice wine (usually 8–10 percent proof) used only for cooking. It is pale, with a slightly syrupy texture.

Miso: A paste made from fermented soybeans, it is used for everything from soups and dressings to marinades, dips, and even desserts. There are many types of miso: white (*shiro miso*) is the most commonly used and has a soft, sweet flavor; red or dark (*aka miso*) is richer and saltier; miso made from brown rice (*genmai miso*) is a recent development, and well worth trying.

Noodles: *See* Cellophane noodles, Soba noodles, and Udon noodles.

Nori: Dried seaweed sheets used for wrapping sushi, such as maki (*see* pages 54–61). It is highly nutritious, rich in protein, vitamins, and minerals, including iodine. Nori is also delicious torn up or crumbled and sprinkled over food as a seasoning. Alternatively, blend a sheet in a food processor or blender and add the flakes to toasted sesame seeds to make your own *furikake*.

Oil: The most commonly used oil for cooking in Japan is rice bran oil, but this is hard to find elsewhere, so peanut oil, sunflower oil, or canola oil can be used instead. Light olive oil or a vegetable oil are often used for dressings, but sesame oil, canola oil, grapeseed oil, and hemp oil may be used, too. Using a variety of oils in your diet means that you will get a good balance of healthy fats and antioxidants, such as vitamin E.

Potsu: The generic word for a sauce or sauced dish.

Rice: *See* Sushi rice.

Rice vinegar: Made from brown or white rice, rice vinegar is essential for seasoning sushi rice and is used in many dressings and sauces. It has excellent antibacterial properties, and is also used to preserve cooked sushi rice. Rice vinegar can reduce the GI of the rice you eat, and thereby help to keep energy levels more consistent. When consumed in a pickle at the end of a meal, it reputedly has digestive benefits.

Sake: Japanese rice wine (which is 16–20 percent proof), can be drunk hot or cold and is the perfect drink to accompany sushi. An inexpensive sake is fine for cooking purposes, and a dry sherry can be used instead. Sake has fewer calories than gin or vodka.

Sashimi: Extremely fresh fish or meat that is sliced thinly into bite-size pieces.

Seaweed: *See* Kombu and Nori.

Sesame oil: There are two types—toasted and untoasted. The untoasted oil has a delicate flavor; it can be used for frying but has a low burning point, so be careful. The toasted oil is stronger and is best used as a condiment or for dressings so that its distinctive, nutty flavor isn't destroyed. It can also be poured over dishes to finish them.

Sesame seeds: Black sesame seeds, or toasted white sesame seeds, are great for sprinkling over salads, meat, or fish to give them extra texture and crunch. The toasted variety may be hard to find in supermarkets, but it's easy to toast the seeds yourself in a dry skillet, and doing so does make a real flavor difference. As well as tasting nutty and delicious, sesame seeds help to

lower cholesterol and strengthen the blood vessels, and they are a great source of calcium, magnesium, iron, and zinc.

Shichimi: Also known as "seven-flavor chili pepper," this is a hot, spiced powder used for sprinkling over dishes to add some fragrant heat. It usually contains a mixture of ground chili powder, ground sanshō, citrus zest, sesame seeds, hemp seeds, ginger, and *nori*. As an alternative, you could use dried red pepper flakes instead.

Shiitake mushrooms: Fresh shiitake have a deep, meaty flavor and are readily available in large supermarkets. Dried shiitake can be used instead; just reconstitute them in boiling water for 20 minutes.

Shiso: A green or red herb, sometimes called "perilla," which is a member of the mint family. It has many uses, and is a constituent of *furikake* seasoning.

Soba noodles: Often made from a mixture of wheat and buckwheat flour, these noodles can also be 100 percent buckwheat, which makes them gluten-free. Bought dried, they are thin, like spaghetti, and are cooked in exactly the same way—for a few minutes in boiling water. They can be eaten hot with broth, or cold as a salad. Noodles, both *udon* and soba, but especially the buckwheat ones, are low GI, which means they release energy slowly and steadily—much better than quick sugar highs.

Soybeans: *See* Edamame.

Soy sauce: One of the most important ingredients in Japanese cooking, this sauce is made from fermented soybeans and replaces salt in many recipes. Dark soy, which is used more often than light soy, is slightly richer and sweeter, but less salty.

Sugar alternatives: Agave, coconut sugar, fruit sugar, stevia, and xylitol are all good alternatives to white granulated sugar. Brown sugar alternatives include brown rice syrup, date sugar, honey, maple syrup, or jaggery (palm sugar).

Sushi-grade fish: This simply means very fresh seafood from safe, reliable sources. Sushi-grade tuna, for example, has often been blast-frozen for 30 minutes at source to destroy any potential bacteria or parasites. It's always advisable to use a good fish dealer if you want to find really fresh fish for making sushi. Supermarkets now stock excellent-quality fish, but may not be able to offer "sushi-grade" because the term is a general description rather than a precise definition. At itsu, we care about sustainability, and all our tuna is supported by the Sustainable Fisheries Partnership's FishSource database (www.fishsource.com).

Sushi rice: Short-grain rice, also known as Japanese rice or glutinous rice, used for sushi. When cooked, this is stickier and softer than long-grain rice, and can be formed into shapes that hold together well. Brown short-grain rice is a good alternative to the usual white polished variety because it contains more valuable nutrients. Rice is gluten-free, contains energizing complex carbohydrates and virtually no fat.

Tahini: A paste made from ground sesame seeds. Asian sesame paste is often made using unhulled seeds, so it has a darker color and coarser texture than that used in Greek, Turkish, and Middle Eastern cooking. The latter type, which is lighter and smoother, is easier to find in the supermarkets. Either variety can be used in our recipes.

Tamari: A wheat-free alternative to *soy sauce*. High in protein, magnesium, potassium, and iron, it can be used instead of soy in all the recipes if you are gluten intolerant.

Tobiko: Red/orange flying fish roe. It has a mildly salty taste and crunchy texture, and is used on the outside of some sushi rolls. It is also excellent as one of the ingredients inside a hand roll (*see* page 64). A good alternative is salmon roe, although the eggs are slightly larger.

Tofu: Also known as bean curd, tofu is made from cooked soybeans pressed into blocks. It can be soft/silken with a texture similar to custard (good for dressings and sauces) or firm/cotton (good for slicing). It is a great alternative to meat, eggs, or dairy produce and is suitable for vegetarians, vegans, and those who are lactose intolerant.

Udon noodles: Thick wheat noodles, often served in a broth. You can buy them dried or precooked (instant).

Umami: The fifth taste sensation in addition to sweet, sour, bitter, and salty. Umami describes the deeply savory or "meaty" flavors

found in foods containing glutamate, a naturally occurring amino acid. These foods include mushrooms, ripe tomatoes, soy sauce, and preserved fish—anchovies and dried bonito flakes, for example—as well as cured meats and Parmesan cheese.

Wakame: Means "sesame seaweed," which gives you an idea of the flavor. It can be bought dried and shredded, and reconstituted in cold water in only 5 minutes. Often used in salads and many miso-based soups, it is rich in iodine, which is important for a healthy thyroid gland.

Wasabi: A horseradish-like plant that is native to Japan and grows in fresh mountain streams. It is hard to find fresh wasabi in the United States (and it can be expensive), but you can use the cheaper and more readily available powdered form (add water and make a paste) or buy it premixed in tubes. Both are hot, so it must be added carefully. Fresh horseradish can be used as an alternative.

Yuzu: A fruit that looks like a small, knobbly grapefruit and tastes tart but sweet, similar to a mandarin. It is difficult to find fresh yuzu in the United States, but bottles of Yutaka brand yuzu juice can be bought online or from good Japanese food stores. Alternatively, use mandarin juice mixed with a little lemon and lime juice. Yuzu is a wonderfully antioxidant citrus fruit, containing three times more vitamin C than a lemon.

USEFUL EQUIPMENT

Bamboo steamer: For cooking vegetables, because steaming preserves more of the nutrients than boiling.

Blender: A blender with a pitcher or an immersion blender work for all the recipes in this book.

Garlic press: For crushing garlic if you'd prefer to do this than grate it.

Grater: With large holes for grating ginger and small holes suitable for grating garlic.

Heavy saucepan with lid: Essential for making perfect Japanese-style rice.

Measuring spoons and cups: Regular silverware and drinking cups vary in size but standard kitchen measuring spoons and cups give the exact amounts needed. Use these when measuring for best results. For dry ingredients, use the back of a blunt knife to level off the ingredient. To use a liquid measuring cup, make sure the gradients on the cup are at eye level when you measure.

Sharp knives: Essential for cutting fish, and for making all kinds of chopping easier and quicker.

Sushi mat: Made of thin bamboo sticks and essential for making maki rolls.

Timer: For cooking rice with perfect precision.

Pantry essentials

Here are some useful ingredients to keep in stock so that you can make the recipes in this book whenever you want. They all have a long shelf life and most of them are easy to find in large supermarkets. Alternatively, buy them online (*see* page 188) or from good Japanese food stores.

1

1. **Rice vinegar:** Look for brands that sell natural or organic varieties.

2. **Miso paste:** Organic types are available as are some that are GMO free and without MSG. *See* page 12 for varieties available in the supermarket.

3. **Fish sauce:** Look for Thai fish sauce.

4. **Kombu:** Large thick strips of dried seaweed. Used to make dashi stock as well as a seasoning for dressings and sauces. Available online or from Japanese food stores.

5. **Wasabi:** Powdered; available from specialty Japanese food stores and online.

6. **Wakame:** This dried seaweed may be hard to find in supermarkets, so look online or in Japanese food stores.

7. **Tofu:** It's useful to have both soft and firm varieties in your refrigerator.

8. **Bonito flakes:** Flakes of smoked, dried fish used to season stocks and sauces. Available in airtight bags, which store well. Buy them online or from Japanese food stores.

9. **Sushi rice:** A short-grain rice. Look for a "premium quality" brand labeled as sushi rice.

10. **Pickled ginger:** Sold in large supermarkets, Japanese grocery stores, and online.

11. **Mirin:** A sweet rice wine vinegar.

12. **Soy sauce:** We recommend the Kikkoman brand of both soy and gluten-free soy (tamari).

13. **Toasted sesame seeds:** If you can't find these, it's easy to toast ordinary sesame seeds in a hot, dry skillet.

14. **Nori:** Dried seaweed sheets made by Laver are sold in large supermarkets; they are similar to Japanese nori; or look for Japanese nori online.

15. **Rice wrappers:** Rice paper for spring rolls (also known as spring roll wrappers or rice skins) are available from larger supermarkets, Asian supermarkets, or online.

Chicken stock: For instant chicken stock, you can use a concentrated form.

Dashi powder: Instant dashi, also called *hon dashi* or *dashi no moto*, is available online or from Japanese suppliers.

Peanut oil: Or other light cooking oil, such as grapeseed, sunflower, or vegetable oil.

Noodles: Keep a stock of cellophane noodles in two thicknesses (fine, resembling angel hair, and wider, resembling tagliatelle), plus udon and soba noodles.

Sake: Choose an inexpensive variety for cooking, or use dry sherry as an alternative.

Sesame oil: Try to find pure sesame oil instead of toasted; it has a delicately nutty flavor and is delicious in dressings.

Sugar alternatives: Agave, coconut sugar, jaggery (palm sugar), stevia, and xylitol are all good alternatives to granulated sugar.

2

3

USEFUL FRESH INGREDIENTS

Fresh ginger root, garlic, hot red Thai chiles, lemons, limes, and scallions.

SOUPS }

- 93 calories
- 0.7 g saturated fat

Simple miso soup

In Japan, people love miso soup so much that they even eat it for breakfast. We're not stopping you! At itsu, you can even buy packages of premixed miso paste—just add hot water and tofu for a quick version of this soup. Instant dashi (just add boiling water) is also available in neat little packets, so it's easy to keep some in the pantry (see page 188 for suppliers).

Serves 4 as a small bowl

3⅓ cups instant dashi, Homemade Dashi Stock (*see* page 165), or water

3 tablespoons white miso paste

3½ oz firm tofu, cut into cubes

large pinch of dried wakame, soaked in cold water for 5 minutes, then drained

2 scallions, sliced

1   Bring the stock to a simmer. Put the miso in a small bowl and mix in a tablespoon of the hot stock to soften it slightly and make a smooth liquid paste. Stir the paste into the stock until dissolved.

2   Put the tofu and wakame in the bottom of 4 serving bowls and pour the hot soup over them. Sprinkle with the scallions to serve.

{ **Nutritional tip:** Miso is a paste made from fermented soybeans, and it is rich in probiotic bacteria, which means it's good for intestinal health.

Variation: Try foamed soy milk as a topping for a miso cappuccino.

- 269 calories
- 3.9 g saturated fat

Smoked mackerel miso soup

Add a smoky note to a simple miso soup—and some extra health benefits, too.

Serves 4 as an appetizer or 2 as a main course

3⅓ cups instant dashi, Homemade Dashi Stock (*see* page 165), or water

3 tablespoons white miso paste

3½ oz smoked mackerel, skinned and flaked into small pieces

3½ oz firm tofu, cut into cubes

large pinch of dried wakame, soaked in cold water for 5 minutes, then drained

1 scallion, sliced

1   Bring the stock to a simmer. Put the miso in a small bowl and mix in a tablespoon of the hot stock to soften it slightly and make a smooth liquid paste. Stir the paste into the stock until dissolved.

2   Equally divide the mackerel, tofu, and wakame among serving bowls and pour the hot miso stock over the contents in the bowls. Sprinkle with the scallion and serve piping hot.

{ **Nutritional tip:** Mackerel is one of the finest sources of omega-3 oils, which fight inflammation and help to keep the heart and brain healthy.

Variation: Turn the soup into more of a meal by adding sliced shiitake mushrooms, leeks, or baby spinach leaves.

Simple miso soup

- 45 calories
- 3 g saturated fat

Dynamite broth
We never use dashi that contains monosodium glutamate (MSG) when we make this soup at itsu. We think this flavor-enhancing chemical is unnecessary, so if you decide to buy dashi instead of make it, do look out for one that's MSG-free. We use dashi as the basis of potsu (sauce) recipes, as well as in our Detox Soup (see page 24). The broth will keep for up to a week in the refrigerator, and also freezes well, so you can always have some on hand to make a quick soup.

Serves 4

6¾ cups instant dashi, Homemade Dashi Stock
(see page 165), or water

⅓ cup white miso paste

2 tablespoons coconut milk

1 tablespoon mirin

1½-inch piece of fresh ginger root, grated (about 3 tablespoons)

1 teaspoon tamarind paste

1 garlic clove, grated or crushed

4 lime leaves, chopped

1 hot red Thai chile, finely chopped

1   Bring the stock to a simmer. Put the miso in a small bowl and mix in a tablespoon of the hot stock to soften it slightly and make a smooth liquid paste. Stir the paste into the stock until dissolved.

2   Put all the remaining ingredients into a blender and blend to combine. Pour into the hot stock and simmer for about 5 minutes to let the flavors develop. (If you don't have a blender, just chop the vegetables into smaller pieces at the beginning and omit this step.)

3   Use immediately or cool and store in the refrigerator for up to a week.

- 200 calories
- 1.7 g saturated fat

Detox soup

A favorite itsu lunchtime soup, this is full of delicious vegetables and noodles. You'll get two antioxidant-packed vegetable portions, and a good amount of satisfying protein from each bowl. It's hard to find a healthier way to fill up! If you prefer, you can use a handful of each vegetable, prepared, instead of measuring it.

Serves 4

1 quantity Dynamite Broth (*see* page 23)

1 red bell pepper, cored and seeded

1 cup or a handful of trimmed green beans

2 small carrots

2 cups or a handful of snow peas

3½ oz or a handful of shiitake mushrooms

3½ cups or a handful of spinach

1 cup or a handful of bean sprouts

7 oz firm tofu, cut into cubes

3 tablespoons wakame, soaked in cold water for 5 minutes, then drained

1½ oz thin cellophane noodles, soaked in boiling water for 5 minutes, then drained

Nutritional tip: Wakame is a type of seaweed that is rich in iodine, which is important for a healthy thyroid gland; the tofu in this soup also adds lean protein, good for filling you without piling on the pounds.

1   Bring the broth to a simmer. Meanwhile, cut all the vegetables, apart from the spinach and bean sprouts, into bite-size pieces.

2   Add all the chopped vegetables and boil for 2½ minutes, then add the spinach and bean sprouts for 30 seconds.

3   Put the tofu, wakame, and noodles in the bottom of each bowl and ladle the vegetables and hot broth over the contents in the bowls.

- 300 calories
- 2.7 g saturated fat

Easy chicken pho

This noodle dish, eaten all across Vietnam, is growing so popular in Western countries that there's even a restaurant chain named after it. The recipe is a refreshingly skinny blend of fragrant spices and herbs in a healthy ginger-infused broth. With juicy chicken pieces, naturally gluten-free glass noodles, and crisp bean sprouts, this is a dish that's true to our aim and butterfly light.

Serves 2

1 white onion, halved

1½-inch piece of fresh ginger root, thickly sliced

3⅓ cups chicken stock

1 teaspoon coriander seeds

4 cloves

2 star anise

½ cinnamon stick

small bunch of cilantro

2 boneless, skinless chicken thighs

2 teaspoons jaggery or brown sugar alternative

1 tablespoon Thai fish sauce

salt

TO SERVE

2 oz flat rice noodles, soaked in boiling water for 15 minutes (or according to package directions)

2 large handfuls of bean sprouts

1 red onion, finely sliced

a big handful of mixed cilantro (reserved from small bunch above), basil, and mint leaves, coarsely chopped

1 hot red Thai chile, finely chopped

juice of ½ lime

1   Heat a dry, heavy skillet until hot. Char the onion and ginger in it for 4 minutes each side. This adds a wonderful depth of flavor, but if you're in a hurry, you can skip this step.

2   Put the stock in a saucepan with the onion, ginger, spices, and cilantro stems (reserve the leaves) and bring to a boil. Add the chicken thighs and cook for 15 minutes. Lift the chicken out with a slotted spoon and let cool slightly before slicing into bite-size pieces.

3   Strain the stock into a bowl, discarding the solids, then return to the pan. Add salt to taste, then the sugar, fish sauce, and chicken pieces.

4   To serve, put the rice noodles into bowls and ladle the hot stock and chicken over them. Sprinkle with the bean sprouts, red onion, herbs, chile, and lime juice, or offer these separately for the diners to add themselves.

Nutritional tip: Fresh cilantro contains as much vitamin C as citrus fruit.

- 189 calories
- 8.2 g saturated fat

Squash, spinach & coconut soup with ginger

Full of goodness and warmth, this soup is quick and easy to make, and it can be a great vegetarian option, too— just use vegetable stock instead of chicken. The creamy coconut, soothing ginger, and crunch of bamboo shoots make it very satisfying.

Serves 4

4¼ cups chicken stock

¾ cup coconut milk

1 hot red Thai chile, finely chopped

1½-inch piece of fresh ginger root, finely chopped (about 3 tablespoons)

1 tablespoon soy sauce

1 tablespoon Thai fish sauce

2 teaspoons lemon juice

1 teaspoon cornstarch

½ butternut squash, seeded and cut into ½-inch cubes

about 9 cups spinach leaves

about 1 cup bamboo shoots, rinsed, or 12 ears baby corn, chopped

1   Bring the stock to a boil in a large saucepan and add the coconut milk, chile, ginger, soy sauce, and fish sauce.

2   Mix the lemon juice with the cornstarch in a bowl to form a smooth paste. Stir the paste into the stock and cook at a gentle boil for 5 minutes.

3   Add the squash to the stock and continue to boil gently for 5–7 minutes, until tender.

4   Stir in the spinach and cook for another minute, or until just wilted.

5   Blend briefly to make a deliciously creamy soup with a slightly chunky texture. (If you don't have a blender, just chop the vegetables into smaller pieces at the beginning and omit this step.)

6   Finally, stir in the bamboo shoots or baby corn and heat through to serve.

- 117 calories
- 1.9 g saturated fat

Egg drop soup with shiitake mushrooms Incredibly

easy to put together, this is a favorite pantry dinner among young Japanese—and it's great on a budget, too. It provides all the nutrients you need and is full of flavor and wonderfully satisfying.

Serves 2

2 cups instant dashi, Homemade Dashi Stock (*see* page 165), or water

3½ oz shiitake mushrooms, finely chopped ....

2 eggs

1 tablespoon soy sauce, plus extra to serve (optional)

1 tablespoon mirin

sprigs of cilantro, to garnish (optional)

Variations: Dried shiitake can be used instead of fresh, but remember to soak them first for 20 minutes in boiling water. Alternatively, use edamame (soybeans), or other small vegetables, such as peas or chopped asparagus.

1 Bring the stock to a boil. Add the mushrooms and cook for 3 minutes.

2 Whisk the eggs with the soy sauce and mirin, then stir into the stock. They will form beautiful strands in the hot liquid.

3 Serve piping hot garnished with cilantro sprigs, if desired, with extra soy sauce as seasoning, if required.

- 194 calories
- 1.4 g saturated fat

Hot & sour soup with pork & noodles

Low in calories but really filling, this is a great soup to take into the office and reheat for lunch. Any leftovers are great for a quick, ready-to-heat dinner.

Serves 4

3½ oz mixed mushrooms (shiitake, oyster, or enoki work well)

3½ oz thin cellophane noodles, soaked in boiling water for 5 minutes, then drained

3½ oz ground pork

2 scallions, sliced

a small handful of cilantro, chopped

lime wedges (optional)

BROTH

6⅓ cups chicken stock

½ teaspoon salt

1 hot red Thai chile, sliced in half lengthwise

1 teaspoon jaggery or brown sugar alternative

juice of 1 lime

1 lemon grass stalk, finely chopped

4 lime leaves

2 tablespoons Thai fish sauce

1 First make the broth. Bring the stock to a boil, then add all the other broth ingredients and simmer for a few minutes to steep.

2 Add the mushrooms, noodles, and pork, stirring well to break up the meat, and cook for 3–4 minutes.

3 Serve with the scallions and cilantro sprinkled on top and, if you desire, with a wedge of lime on the side.

Variation: Try making this with shrimp instead of pork—a delicious (and still skinny) alternative.

- 182 calories
- 1 g saturated fat

Hot & sour shrimp soup
The delicious fragrant flavors of lemon grass, lime, and hot chile make this a fully balanced yet pure-tasting soup.

Serves 2

3⅓ cups chicken stock

½ teaspoon salt

½–1 hot red Thai chile (depending on preference)

1 teaspoon jaggery or brown sugar alternative

3 tablespoons lime juice

1 lemon grass stalk, finely chopped

4 lime leaves

2 tablespoons Thai fish sauce

3½ oz shiitake mushrooms, sliced

5 oz uncooked peeled shrimp

TO SERVE

2 scallions, finely chopped

sprigs of cilantro

lime wedges

1   Bring the stock to a boil. Add all the other ingredients except the shrimp, and simmer for 5 minutes.

2   Add the shrimp and cook for 2 minutes, until they turn pink.

3   Ladle the soup into bowls and serve with the scallions and cilantro on top, plus a lime wedge alongside for extra zing.

- 222 calories
- 2.3 g saturated fat

Hot & sour lemon grass chicken soup

Here's a fragrant soup that is hot, sour, salty, and sweet all at once. It's filling, healthy, and easy to make. itsu chefs prefer chicken thigh in soups and potsus because it's juicer than breast and gives a better flavor.

Serves 4

6⅓ cups chicken stock

1 teaspoon jaggery or brown sugar alternative

1½-inch piece of fresh ginger root, sliced

1 lemon grass stalk, chopped

2 shallots, sliced

4 lime leaves

1 teaspoon tamarind paste

2 boneless, skinless chicken thighs

juice of 1 lime

2 tablespoons Thai fish sauce

1 hot red Thai chile, seeded and coarsely chopped (optional)

small bunch of cilantro, coarsely chopped

1 Put the stock into a saucepan with the sugar, ginger, lemon grass, shallots, lime leaves, and tamarind paste. Bring to a boil, then add the chicken and simmer for 15 minutes.

2 Using a slotted spoon, remove the chicken from the stock and set aside to cool slightly. Strain the stock, discarding the solids, then return it to the saucepan.

3 When cool enough to handle, shred or slice the chicken into bite-size pieces and add to the stock with the lime juice, fish sauce, chile (if using), and cilantro. Ladle into bowls to serve.

- 224 calories
- 9.7 g saturated fat

Chicken, mushroom & coconut soup

This velvety blend of chicken and creamy coconut is deeply satisfying but skinny, too, and any leftovers will keep well in the refrigerator.

Serves 4

4¼ cups chicken stock

¾ cup coconut milk ....

1 hot red Thai chile, seeded and finely chopped

7 oz mixed mushrooms (shiitake, oyster, enoki, or buna shimeji work well)

4 lime leaves

5 oz boneless, skinless chicken thighs

a small handful each of bok choy, sugarsnap peas, spinach, and baby corn

1 tablespoon Thai fish sauce

1 teaspoon jaggery or brown sugar alternative

1 tablespoon lime juice

small bunch of cilantro, coarsely chopped, to serve

Nutritional tip: Coconut is a great source of iron, potassium, and zinc. Like seeds and avocado, coconut milk is naturally high in saturated fat, but it is mostly in the form of medium-chain saturated fatty acids (MCFAs), particularly lauric acid. MCFAs are used up more quickly by the body than other saturated fats and are less likely to be stored as fat.

1   Heat the stock in a saucepan with the coconut milk, chile, mushrooms, and lime leaves. Bring to a boil, then add the chicken and simmer for 10–15 minutes.

2   Using a slotted spoon, remove the chicken from the stock and set aside to cool slightly. When cool enough to handle, finely slice the chicken into bite-size pieces.

3   Return the chicken to the stock and add the vegetables, fish sauce, sugar, and lime juice. Cook for just a few more minutes, until the vegetables soften but still have a little bite.

4   Ladle into bowls and sprinkle with the chopped cilantro to serve.

RICE, NOODLES, SUSHI & EGGS }

- 238 calories
- 0.7 g saturated fat

Japanese-style rice with scallion & ginger sauce

This fabulous rice dish is inspired by a recipe in David Chang's great book *Momofuku*. If you've never seen it, get your hands on one soon—it's kick-ass! You can use the sauce with everything from noodles and brown rice to salads and grilled chicken or fish.

Serves 4 as a side dish or small plate

⅔ cup peas, fresh or frozen

2 scallions, thinly sliced

¾-inch piece of fresh ginger root, grated (about 2 tablespoons)

1 tablespoon light oil, such as peanut

2 tablespoons store-bought sushi rice seasoning vinegar, or make your own (*see* Tip, page 44)

1 quantity Easy Japanese-style Rice (*see* page 44)

salt

1 Cook the peas in boiling salted water for 2–3 minutes, depending on whether they're fresh or frozen, then drain.

2 Put the scallions, ginger, oil, and sushi rice seasoning vinegar into a bowl or blender and mix well or blend briefly to make a sauce.

3 Stir the peas into the sauce, then fold into the rice.

42

- 270 calories
- trace saturated fat

Easy Japanese-style rice
Perfectly seasoned Japanese-style rice is really easy to make. All you need is a small saucepan with a lid, and a timer helps, too. Use this delicious, seasoned, sticky rice for sushi, as a side dish, or as a base for the Broiled Chicken Teriyaki or Salmon Teriyaki (*see* pages 120 and 136). It freezes well, too, so make a double quantity and keep the rest for another time. (The amounts below make about 1¾ cups cooked rice.)

Serves 4 as a small plate

¾ cup uncooked Japanese-style short-grain rice

¾ cup water, filtered if possible

1 tablespoon store-bought sushi rice seasoning vinegar, or make your own (*see* below)

1   Wash the rice in cold tap water until the water runs clear. This should take a couple of rinses. Drain and set aside for at least 15 minutes.

2   Put the rice into a saucepan and add the filtered water. Cover and bring to a boil for 1–2 minutes, then reduce the heat and simmer for 12 minutes. Turn off the heat and let stand, still covered, for 10 minutes.

3   Wet a flat tray and spread the rice over it. Sprinkle with the sushi rice seasoning vinegar and stir gently but thoroughly with a wooden spoon, lifting and folding the rice to help it cool slightly and absorb the seasoning. If you want to be really Japanese about it, you can fan it to help it cool.

Tip: Homemade sushi rice seasoning vinegar is easy to make yourself. Simply mix together 1 teaspoon rice vinegar, 2 teaspoons mirin, ½ teaspoon sugar, and ½ teaspoon salt. (These quantities make 1 tablespoon of seasoning, but can be multiplied proportionally to make as much as you prefer. If stored in a screw-top jar, the seasoning will keep for at least a month.)

Variations: Pimp up a plain rice side dish with furikake or soy-toasted seeds (*see* page 89), or make our famously good scallion and ginger sauce (*see* page 42).

- 141 calories
- 0.3 g saturated fat

Brown rice for sushi As an even

healthier sushi option, try using brown rice. Unlike polished white rice, brown rice still contains all its valuable nutrients, giving us the full benefit of its fiber, vitamins, and blood sugar stabilizing properties.

Serves 4 as a side dish or small plate

¾ cup uncooked Japanese-style short-grain brown rice

1 cup water, filtered if possible

1 tablespoon store-bought sushi rice seasoning vinegar, or make your own (*see* Tip, opposite)

1   Wash the rice in cold tap water until the water runs clear, then drain and set aside for at least 15 minutes.

2   Put the rice into a saucepan and add the filtered water. Cover and bring to a boil for 1–2 minutes, then reduce the heat and simmer for 30 minutes. Turn off the heat and let stand, still covered, for 10 minutes.

3   Wet a flat tray and spread the rice over it. Sprinkle with the sushi rice seasoning vinegar and stir gently but thoroughly with a wooden spoon, lifting and folding the rice to help it cool slightly and absorb the seasoning.

- 233 calories
- 2.6 g saturated fat

Seven veg & brown rice potsu with ithai sauce
The base of brown and wild rice makes this recipe a great low-GI favorite to have at home or take to work—a deliciously filling yet belly-light meal, bursting with nutrients. It's also packed with vitamins and antioxidants from the veg mixture, which counts as half of your five-a-day. Any leftovers will keep in the refrigerator for up to two days and can be reheated for another meal, but remember that cooked rice should be reheated only once.

Serves 4

¾ cup mixed brown and wild rice

1 large carrot, trimmed and cut into fine sticks

1 red bell pepper, cored, seeded, and sliced

1 leek, trimmed, cleaned, and sliced

1½ cups broccoli florets

1 cup or a handful of trimmed green beans

1½ cups or a handful of sugarsnap peas

3½ cups or a handful of spinach

1 quantity ithai Sauce (*see* page 173)

salt

1 Wash the rice thoroughly and cover it with warm water. Set aside to soak for at least 10 minutes.

2 Bring a large saucepan of water to a boil, add a good pinch of salt, and cook all the vegetables except for the spinach for 3 minutes. Add the spinach 30 seconds before the end of the cooking time.

3 Reserve the cooking water and, using a slotted spoon, transfer all the vegetables to a colander and set aside to drain, covering to keep warm.

4 Drain the rice, then add it to the vegetable water (which will now be full of nutrients) and boil it for 15 minutes, or according to the package directions. Drain well and divide among bowls. Spoon the warm vegetables on top and serve with the ithai sauce.

- 300 calories
- 3.8 g saturated fat

Broiled chicken & brown rice potsu with ithai sauce
Juicy pieces of broiled chicken on nutrient-packed brown rice plus a mountain of vegetables topped with itsu's famous ithai sauce—what could be better?

Serves 4

¾ cup mixed brown and wild rice

5 oz boneless, skinless chicken thighs

1 teaspoon light oil, such as peanut, for coating

1 large carrot, trimmed and cut into fine sticks

1 red bell pepper, cored, seeded, and sliced

1 cup or a handful of trimmed green beans

1½ cups or a handful of snow peas

3½ oz or a handful of shiitake mushrooms, halved

3½ cups or a handful of spinach

1 cup or a handful of bean sprouts

1 quantity ithai Sauce (*see* page 173)

salt and black pepper

1. Wash the rice thoroughly and cover with warm water. Set aside to soak for at least 10 minutes.

2. Heat the broiler to its highest setting. Put the chicken thighs in a roasting pan, season well with salt and black pepper, and coat with the oil. Broil for 10 minutes, turning halfway through the cooking time. Remove and let cool slightly before cutting the chicken into pieces.

3. Meanwhile, bring a large saucepan of water to a boil, add a good pinch of salt, and cook all the vegetables except for the spinach and bean sprouts for 3 minutes. Add the spinach and bean sprouts 30 seconds before the end of the cooking time. Drain well and cover to keep warm.

4. Drain the rice and add it to the vegetable water, which will now be full of nutrients, and boil for 15 minutes, or according to the package directions. Drain well.

5. Put the rice into serving bowls and top with the chicken pieces and vegetables. Pour the ithai sauce over each one and serve with the remaining sauce on the side.

{ **Variations:** Try different vegetables, perhaps leeks, baby broccoli or broccolini, or bok choy, with edamame (soybeans). Furikake or sesame seeds, preferably toasted, or Toasted Pumpkin Seed Topping (*see* page 171) can be sprinkled on the finished dish to garnish, but just 1 tablespoon will add another 34 calories and 0.6g saturated fat to the whole dish.

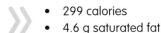

- 299 calories
- 4.6 g saturated fat

Broiled chicken & noodle potsu with dynamite broth

At itsu we top our potsus with pickled kombu, a dark green seaweed that gives them extra crunch. It is available from Asian food stores, but if you have difficulty getting hold of it, use pumpkin seeds or Pickled Cucumber with Ginger (*see* page 93). This yummy, healthy dinner dish is a great reason to keep some Dynamite Broth in the refrigerator.

Serves 4

7 oz boneless, skinless chicken thighs

½ teaspoon light oil, such as peanut, for coating

1 large carrot, trimmed and cut into fine sticks

1 red bell pepper, cored, seeded, and sliced

1 cup or a handful of trimmed green beans

1½ cups or a handful of snow peas

3½ oz or a handful of shiitake mushrooms, halved

3½ cups or a handful of spinach

1 cup or a handful of bean sprouts

1 quantity Dynamite Broth (*see* page 23)

9 oz instant udon noodles or 5 oz dried udon noodles

salt and black pepper

2 tablespoons furikake or sesame seeds, preferably toasted, or Toasted Pumpkin Seed Topping (*see* page 171), to garnish

1   Heat the broiler to its highest setting. Put the chicken thighs in a roasting pan, season well with salt and black pepper, and coat with the oil. Broil for 10 minutes, turning halfway through the cooking time. Remove and let cool slightly before cutting the chicken into bite-size pieces.

2   Meanwhile, bring a large saucepan of water to a boil, add a good pinch of salt, and cook all the vegetables except for the spinach and bean sprouts for 3 minutes. Add the spinach and bean sprouts 30 seconds before the end of the cooking time. Drain well and cover to keep warm.

3   Heat the dynamite broth in a saucepan. Meanwhile, cook the noodles in boiling water according to the package directions. Drain and divide the noodles among serving bowls.

4   Put the vegetables and chicken on top of the noodles, then pour the hot broth over them. Sprinkle furikake or sesame seeds, preferably toasted, or toasted pumpkin seeds on top of each bowl.

Tip: Several parts of this recipe can be prepared in advance. The noodles can be cooked and dressed with a little peanut oil to prevent them from sticking together. The vegetable mixture can also be precooked and stored in the refrigerator until needed. Warm through before just serving.

- 289 calories
- 3.6 g saturated fat

Seven veg & udon potsu with dynamite broth

A mountain of vegetables on a bed of steaming noodles with our famous Dynamite Broth. Dried udon are slightly skinnier, have a firmer texture than other noodles, and store well.

Serves 4

1 large carrot, trimmed and cut into fine sticks

1 red bell pepper, cored, seeded, and sliced

1 cup or a handful of trimmed green beans

1½ cups or a handful of snow peas

3½ oz or a handful of shiitake mushrooms, halved

3½ cups or a handful of spinach

1 cup or a handful of bean sprouts

1 quantity Dynamite Broth (see page 23)

5 oz dried udon noodles or 7 oz instant udon noodles

salt

3 tablespoons Toasted Pumpkin Seed Topping (see page 171), to garnish

1   Bring a large saucepan of water to a boil, add a good pinch of salt, and cook all the vegetables except for the spinach and bean sprouts for 3 minutes. Add the spinach and bean sprouts for the last 30 seconds of the cooking time. Drain well and cover to keep warm.

2   Heat the dynamite broth in a saucepan.

3   Meanwhile, cook the noodles in boiling water according to the package directions.

4   Drain and divide the noodles among serving bowls. Put the vegetables on top and pour the hot broth over them. Sprinkle with the pumpkin seeds to serve.

- 247 calories
- 1.1 g saturated fat

Hot soba noodles in mushroom broth
A butterfly-light but flavor-filled broth full of nutrient-dense fresh and dried mushrooms and light soba noodles. Imagine a plate of pasta without the calories.

Serves 2

4¼ cups instant dashi, Homemade Dashi Stock (*see* page 165), or water

⅓ oz dried shiitake or any other strongly flavored dried mushrooms

2 tablespoons soy sauce

1 teaspoon rice vinegar

1 tablespoon mirin

3½ oz mixture of fresh mushrooms, sliced or cut into small pieces (such as shiitake, oyster, enoki, or buna shimeji—available from larger supermarkets or Asian food stores)

2½ oz dried soba noodles ....

2 scallions, finely chopped, to garnish

salt

Nutritional tip: Soba noodles are made from buckwheat flour, which is gluten-free and full of rutin, a bioflavanoid that extends the action of vitamin C and acts as an antioxidant. Buckwheat is also high in magnesium, which helps with energy production. These noodles will keep your blood sugar levels steadier than many other carbohydrates.

1 Pour the stock into a saucepan and bring to a boil. Add the dried mushrooms and simmer for 10 minutes.

2 Strain the stock and chop the mushrooms finely. Return both to the pan and add the soy sauce, vinegar, mirin, and fresh mushrooms. Simmer for 5 minutes.

3 Meanwhile, cook the noodles in boiling salted water for 7 minutes, or according to the package directions. Drain and divide between 2 bowls. Ladle the stock and mushrooms over the noodles, then sprinkle with the scallions to garnish.

Step-by-step sushi "Sushi" is a general term used to describe rice seasoned with vinegar and combined with other ingredients.

There are numerous styles and forms of sushi, but we've chosen just a few of the best to get you started.

Maki are rolled sushi—rice rolled around a filling with a sheet of nori on the outside (*hosomaki* or *futomaki*), or with nori rolled around the filling and rice on the outside of the roll (*uramaki*).

Nigiri are flattened sushi—small oblongs of hand-pressed rice with a topping laid over them.

Temaki or **hand rolls** are simple cone shapes. These are best made just before you eat them so that the nori stays crisp and holds its shape. They're loads of fun to make with a group of friends; just lay out all the ingredients and get everyone rolling their own.

Note: The Japanese don't use chopsticks to eat sushi—they pick the pieces up with their fingers.

How to make maki with rice inside The neat little rolls are easy to master, consisting simply of a filling rolled inside a sheet of seaweed. You might want to practice with just rice at first in order to get the hang of the rolling technique.

TO MAKE 12 MAKI YOU WILL NEED

1 sheet of nori

½ cup or 2 small handfuls of cooked Easy Japanese-style Rice (*see* page 44)

your chosen filling (*see* pages 56–57 for inspiration)

1   Place the nori sheet on a work surface with the lines running vertically. Fold the sheet in half lengthwise, then tear or cut along the fold so you have 2 rectangles.

2   Lay 1 rectangle on a sushi mat. Arrange the other ingredients around the mat, and place a bowl of warm water alongside. Wet your fingers in the water, then press half the rice over the nori, leaving a clear ¾-inch border along the top edge.

3   Arrange your chosen filling neatly on the rice along the edge nearest to you.

4   Lift the edge of the mat and roll it away from you, using your thumbs while holding the filling in place with your fingers. Continue lifting the mat until the filled nori forms a roll underneath it. Dab a little water on the clear border of the nori and press to seal it. Chop the ends off to neaten and cut the finished roll into 6 equal pieces. Repeat this process with the remaining half sheet of nori.

- 196 calories
- 0.4 g saturated fat

Spicy tuna fish maki
Finely chopped pickled ginger inside these little rice rolls gives them that extra-special zing.

Makes 12

1 sheet of nori

¾ cup (about 2 handfuls) cooked Easy Japanese-style Rice (*see* page 44)

1½ oz very fresh tuna, cut into long strips

2 tablespoons prepared pickled ginger, finely chopped

TO SERVE (OPTIONAL)

soy sauce

wasabi paste

1   Follow steps 1 and 2 on page 54.

2   Put a strip of tuna along the edge of the rice nearest you and cover with a layer of the pickled ginger.

3   Roll up the nori and cut into pieces as shown in step 4 on page 54.

4   Repeat all these steps with the remaining ingredients.

5   Serve with soy sauce and wasabi paste for dipping, if liked.

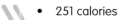

- 251 calories
- 2 g saturated fat

Salmon & avocado maki An all-time
favorite at itsu, these fresh salmon, creamy avocado, and crunchy cucumber rolls
are one of our best sellers.

Makes 12

1 sheet of nori

¾ cup (about 2 handfuls) cooked Easy Japanese-style Rice (*see* page 44)

1½ oz fresh salmon, cut into 2½-inch-long strips

½ ripe avocado, thinly sliced

6 cucumber batons, about 3½ inches long and ¼ inch wide, peeled and seeded

TO SERVE (OPTIONAL)

soy sauce

wasabi paste

1 Follow steps 1 and 2 on page 54.

2 Put a strip of salmon along the edge of the rice nearest you and cover with strips of avocado and cucumber.

3 Roll up the nori and cut into pieces as shown in step 4 on page 54.

4 Repeat all these steps with the remaining ingredients.

5 Serve with soy sauce and wasabi paste for dipping, if liked.

How to make maki with rice outside

We might describe this as an inside-out version of the previous maki because in this case the nori-covered filling is in the middle of the roll with the rice around the outside.

TO MAKE 12 MAKI YOU WILL NEED

1 sheet of nori

1 cup or 4 small handfuls of cooked Easy Japanese-style Rice (see page 44)

1 tablespoon sesame seeds, preferably toasted

your chosen filling (see pages 60–61 for inspiration)

1   Place the nori sheet on a work surface with the lines running vertically. Fold the sheet in half lengthwise, then tear or cut along the fold so you have 2 rectangles.

2   Lay 1 rectangle on a clean board. Arrange the other ingredients around it and place a bowl of warm water alongside. Wet your fingers in the water, then press half the rice over the nori. Sprinkle with half the sesame seeds.

3   Lay a sheet of plastic wrap on a sushi mat. Lift the rice-covered nori sheet and place it rice side down on the plastic wrap. (Don't worry—the rice is sticky, so it won't fall off.) Add your chosen filling, placing it near to the edge of the nori closest to you.

4   Lift the edge of the mat and roll it away from you, using your thumbs while holding the filling in place with your fingers. Continue lifting the mat and the plastic wrap until the filled nori forms a roll underneath them. Dab a little water on the uncovered top edge of the nori to seal it. Chop the ends off to neaten and cut the finished roll into 6 equal pieces. Repeat this process with the remaining half sheet of nori.

- 287 calories
- 2.6 g saturated fat

Crab California maki You need only a teeny

amount of crab for these rolls, so use any leftovers to make Crab Crystal Rolls (*see* page 157), or eat it the next day on rice crackers with avocado and cilantro as a snack.

Makes 12

1 sheet of nori

about 1 cup cooked Easy Japanese-style Rice (*see* page 44)

about 1 tablespoon sesame seeds, preferably toasted

4 teaspoons cooked crabmeat

½ ripe avocado, pitted, peeled, and thinly sliced

12 chives

6 cucumber batons, about 3½ inches long and ¼ inch wide, peeled and seeded

TO SERVE

soy sauce

wasabi paste

1 Follow steps 1–3 on page 58.

2 Put half the crab along the edge of the rice nearest you and cover with half the avocado, chives, and cucumber.

3 Roll up and finish the maki as shown in step 4 on page 58.

4 Repeat all these steps with the remaining ingredients.

5 Serve with soy sauce and wasabi paste for dipping.

Rainbow vegetable maki These maki

look pretty, and they're also suitable for vegetarians because they are fish-free.

Makes 12

1 sheet of nori

about 1 cup (4 small handfuls) cooked Easy Japanese-style Rice (*see* page 44)

about 1 tablespoon sesame seeds, preferably toasted

8 raw fine green beans

½ ripe avocado, pitted, skinned, and thinly sliced

12 chives

6 raw carrot sticks, about 3½ inches long and ¼ inch wide

1 teaspoon Spicy Sauce (*see* page 171, optional)

TO SERVE (OPTIONAL)

soy sauce

wasabi paste

1   Follow steps 1–3 on page 58.

2   Lay two pairs of green beans along the edge of the rice nearest you and cover with half of the avocado, chives, and carrot.

3   Spread half the spicy sauce over the filling, if using.

4   Roll up and finish the maki as shown in step 4 on page 58.

5   Repeat all these steps with the remaining ingredients.

6   Serve with soy sauce and wasabi paste for dipping, if liked.

Variations: Vary the vegetables—try zucchini or cooked squash—or even use soba noodles as a filling. The world is your oyster! Use furikake or flaxseed instead of sesame seeds.

How to make a hand roll
These easy temaki or hand rolls are a great introduction to making sushi. Roll them up and eat them immediately like ice cream cones.

TO MAKE 2 HAND ROLLS YOU WILL NEED

1 sheet of nori

½ cup or 2 small handfuls of cooked Easy Japanese-style Rice (see page 44)

your chosen filling (see page 64 for inspiration)

1   Place the nori sheet on a clean board with the lines running vertically. Fold the sheet in half, then tear or cut along the fold so you have 2 rectangles.

2   Arrange the other ingredients around the nori and place a bowl of warm water alongside. Wet your fingers in the water, then press half the rice over the lower half of 1 nori rectangle.

3   Lay your chosen filling over the rice diagonally.

4   Lift the bottom left-hand corner and fold it toward the diagonally opposite corner of the rice to make a cone shape. Hold the narrowest point of the cone (middle left) and continue rolling tightly toward the top left of the nori. Dab a little water on the nori to seal the finished cone. Repeat steps 2–4 to make the second roll.

- 143 calories
- 2.1 g saturated fat

Salmon hand rolls

Here's a chance to use the technique on page 62, this time with a salmon filling. Once you've got the hang of it, you could use any of the other sushi fillings as alternatives.

Makes 4

2 sheets of nori, cut in half lengthwise (*see* page 62, step 1)

about 1 cup (4 small handfuls) cooked Easy Japanese-style Rice (*see* page 44)

½ teaspoon wasabi paste

4 cucumber batons, about 4¾ inches long and ¼ inch wide, seeded

5 oz skinned salmon fillet, chopped

½ avocado, sliced

1 tablespoon fresh cilantro leaves

¼ cup tobiko (optional)

1 tablespoon sesame seeds, preferably toasted, or furikake

1　Prepare all the ingredients and arrange them around a clean board. (Even better, divide each ingredient into 4 piles ready to go into each roll.) Place a bowl of warm water alongside.

2　Wet your fingers, then press rice onto the nori as described on page 62, step 2. Dab the wasabi over the rice.

3　Place a cucumber stick diagonally across the rice from the top left corner. Put one-quarter of the salmon, avocado, cilantro, and tobiko (if using) on top, then sprinkle with sesame seeds.

4　Roll the nori carefully to make a cone shape as described on page 62, step 4.

5　Repeat, using the rest of the ingredients, to make 3 more cones.

Nutritional tip: Nori is rich in vitamins, and the delicious flavor makes it great to use as a savory wrapping.

- 134 calories
- 0.8 g saturated fat

Salmon sushi
You don't have to be a sushi master to make these flattened sushi, known as nigiri; you don't even need a sushi mat. All that's required is some superfresh fish and a bowl of rice.

Makes 6

2¾ oz very fresh salmon fillet, skinned and cut into 6 thin slices

wasabi paste

⅓ cup cooked Easy Japanese-style Rice (*see* page 44)

TO SERVE

soy sauce

prepared pickled ginger

1   Prepare all the ingredients and arrange them around a clean board. Place a bowl of warm water alongside.

2   Lay a slice of salmon in the palm of one hand and spread a dab of wasabi over it.

3   Wet your fingers in the bowl of water, then take a large pinch of the rice and press it onto the salmon.

4   Put your index finger and ring finger on each side of the rice and your middle finger on top and gently press to shape it into a long rectangle. Squeeze the ends to neaten them.

5   Put the sushi on a plate and repeat with the rest of the fish and rice.

6   Serve with soy sauce and pickled ginger.

{ **Variations:** Try using sea bass, tuna, or sliced scallops instead of salmon.

- 92 calories
- 0.1 g saturated fat

Cooked shrimp sushi These nigiri are great for kids and for pregnant women who can't eat raw fish.

Serves 2

6 large cooked peeled shrimp (about 2 oz), tails left on

⅓ cup cooked Easy Japanese-style Rice (*see* page 44)

wasabi paste

TO SERVE

soy sauce

prepared pickled ginger

1   Prepare all the ingredients and arrange them around a clean board. Place a bowl of warm water alongside.

2   Score the underside of each shrimp so that it uncurls and can be pressed flat. Place a shrimp in the palm of one hand and spread a dab of wasabi over the underside.

3   Wet your fingers in the bowl of water, then take a large pinch of the rice and press it over the wasabi.

4   Put your index finger and ring finger on each side of the rice and your middle finger on top and gently press to shape it into a long rectangle. Squeeze the ends to neaten them.

5   Transfer to a plate, shrimp side up, and repeat the steps with the remaining ingredients. Serve with soy sauce and pickled ginger.

- 244 calories
- 3.6 g saturated fat

Scrambled eggs with shrimp & nori

Here's something easy and healthy to throw together for a quick dinner or when time is short. It's light but filling, tasty, and full of nutrients.

Serves 2

1 teaspoon light oil, such as peanut, for frying

3½ oz cooked or raw peeled shrimp, tails discarded

4 scallions, sliced

4 free-range eggs

3 tablespoons soy sauce

1 sheet of nori, cut into fine strips (scissors are best for this)

1   Heat a skillet, add the oil, then stir-fry the shrimp and scallions for a couple of minutes until the shrimp start to color.

2   Whisk the eggs and soy sauce together and pour into the pan. Lower the heat and cook, stirring and folding, for a couple of minutes until the eggs are just set but still a little creamy.

3   Sprinkle with the nori and stir once more. Spoon onto plates and serve immediately, while the texture is just right.

- 198 calories
- 3.6 g saturated fat

Japanese omelet A perfect skinny and

speedy solution for busy days, this omelet is easy to make and bursting with flavor. Eggs, always free-range, frequently feature on itsu's menu because they are high in protein and nutrients, and low in calories.

Serves 2

4 free-range eggs

1 tablespoon mirin

1 tablespoon soy sauce

1 teaspoon chopped chives, plus a few extra for garnish

1 teaspoon bonito flakes (optional)

1 teaspoon light oil, such as peanut, for frying

soy sauce, for dipping (optional)

chives, to garnish

1   Crack the eggs into a bowl. Add the mirin, soy sauce, chives, and bonito flakes (if using), and whisk well.

2   Heat a skillet, add the oil ,and use a piece of paper towel to spread it around the pan and remove any excess.

3   Pour a ladleful of the egg mixture into the pan and tilt gently so that it coats the bottom. Cook for a few seconds until it starts to set. Using a spatula, lift one side of the omelet and roll or fold it toward one end of the pan.

4   Leaving the rolled omelet in the pan, pour in another ladleful of the egg mixture, lifting the first roll so that the uncooked egg flows underneath it. Cook for a few seconds until slightly set, then roll or fold it back over the thin layer of egg like the first omelet. Repeat this process until all the mixture is used.

5   Transfer to a board and cut into thick pieces so you can see all the layers. Serve with soy sauce for dipping, if liked, and garnish with chives. Alternatively, let cool, then wrap the roll to eat cold as a healthy snack on the run.

VEGETABLES & SALADS }

- 285 calories (plus 160 calories if eaten in flatbread)
- 2.6 g saturated fat (plus 0.3 g if eaten in flatbread)

Baked salmon in miso

Juicy salmon flaked over a bed of healthy vegetables and dressed with a creamy, herb sauce. This can be eaten as a thinning salad or in a warmed flatbread for a delicious, portable lunch. (If you go for the flatbread option, flake the salmon over the other ingredients.)

Serves 2

2 skinned salmon fillets, about 3½ oz each

a large handful of green beans, tops trimmed

a large handful of sugarsnap peas or snow peas

a small handful of edamame (soybeans)

2 handfuls of salad greens, plus grated carrot or chopped radishes for extra crunch (optional)

1 tablespoon Herb Dressing (*see* page 166)

flatbread or pita bread, to serve (optional)

2 teaspoons furikake, or sesame seeds, preferably toasted, or Toasted Pumpkin Seed Topping (*see* page 171)

MARINADE

2 tablespoons miso paste

1 teaspoon water

1 teaspoon soy sauce

1 Preheat the oven to 400°F.

2 Meanwhile, make the marinade by combining all the ingredients for it in a bowl.

3 Place two 8½ x 11-inch pieces of aluminum foil on a work surface and lay a salmon fillet on each. Cover both sides of the salmon with the marinade and wrap loosely in the foil. Place in a roasting pan and bake for 8–10 minutes (a tail fillet will take less time than a thicker fillet).

4 Steam or boil the green beans, sugarsnap peas or snow peas, and edamame (soybeans) for 3 minutes.

5 Dress the salad greens, plus the carrot or radishes (if using), with the herb dressing.

6 Arrange the salad, vegetables, and salmon on 2 flatbreads or pita breads, sprinkle with the toasted seeds, and roll up. Alternatively, divide the salad between 2 plates, top with the vegetables, place the salmon alongside, and sprinkle with the toasted seeds to finish.

Nutritional tip: Just 1 tablespoon of sesame seeds provides around one-tenth of your daily requirement of calcium and magnesium.

- 131 calories (plus 160 calories if eaten in flatbread)
- 1.5 g saturated fat (plus 0.3 g if eaten in flatbread)

Super low-calorie smoked chicken salad

This is the skinniest option in our salad or sandwich range. Quick to assemble and superhealthy to eat, it's packed with protein from the chicken and edamame.

Serves 2

5 oz smoked chicken breast, sliced

2 tablespoons Spicy Sauce (*see* page 171)

⅔ cup edamame (soybeans) or 1 cup trimmed green beans

3½ cups mixed salad greens

¼ cup Herb Dressing (*see* page 166)

flatbread or pita bread, to serve (optional)

1 tablespoon chopped chives

salt

Variations: Ordinary broiled chicken breast can be used instead of smoked chicken. For extra protein, add a hard-boiled egg.

1   Dress the sliced chicken breast with the spicy sauce.

2   Cook the beans in boiling salted water for 3 minutes. Drain and refresh under cold water.

3   Dress the salad greens and beans with the herb dressing. Arrange on 2 flatbreads or pita breads, put the chicken on top, sprinkle with the chives and then roll up. Alternatively, divide the dressed salad between 2 plates, top with the chicken, and sprinkle with the chives to finish.

VEGETABLES & SALADS

Top: Hip & humble hummus salad (*see* page 80); Bottom: Tangy tuna with spicy sauce

- 219 calories (plus 160 calories if eaten in flatbread)
- 1.4 g saturated fat (plus 0.3 g if eaten in flatbread)

Tangy tuna with spicy sauce

Tuna is a "meaty" fish, so it's great for filling you up without being too calorific. The pickled ginger and the spicy sauce give it a wonderful tang, making a simple ingredient taste so delicious you'll want it again and again.

Serves 2

⅔ cup edamame (soybeans), peas, or fava beans

1 (5 oz) can tuna, drained

1 tablespoon prepared pickled ginger, finely chopped, or ¾-inch piece of fresh ginger root, grated (about 2 tablespoons)

1 tablespoon cilantro, chopped

1 tablespoon chives, chopped

3 tablespoons Spicy Sauce (*see* page 171)

a handful of mixed salad greens

1 carrot, cut into fine sticks

2 tablespoons Herb Dressing or Asian Pesto (*see* page 166)

salt

flatbread or pita bread, to serve (optional)

1   Cook the beans or peas in boiling salted water for 3 minutes. Drain and refresh under cold water.

2   Mix the tuna with the ginger, cilantro, chives, spicy sauce, and a pinch of salt.

3   Combine the salad greens with the carrots and dress with the herb dressing or Asian pesto (if you prefer, the dressing can be offered separately). Arrange the salad on a plate and place the beans and tuna mixture on top. Alternatively, place inside flatbreads or pita breads and roll up.

Variations: Serve on a bed of rice, or with a hard-boiled egg for extra protein. The tangy tuna can also be used as a filling for maki (*see* pages 54 and 58).

Tip: When using canned tuna, always make sure that you check its sustainability.

- 291 calories (plus 160 calories if eaten in flatbread)
- 2 g saturated fat (plus 0.3 g if eaten in flatbread)

Hip & humble hummus salad

Spicy, herbed hummus on a bed of salad topped with crunchy seeds is a protein-packed plateful, but it makes a great sandwich filling, too. It's also a good dip to eat with carrot, cucumber, and celery sticks for a healthy snack.

Serves 2

⅔ cup reduced-fat store-bought hummus

1 tablespoon Sriracha chili sauce or 1 teaspoon dried red pepper flakes

1 tablespoon chopped chives

1 tablespoon chopped cilantro

⅔ cup or a large handful of edamame (soybeans)

2 handfuls of mixed salad greens

1 carrot, cut into fine sticks

a small handful of cherry tomatoes

salt

1 tablespoon Toasted Pumpkin Seed Topping, to garnish (*see* page 171)

flatbread or pita bread, to serve (optional)

1   Mix the hummus with the chili sauce and herbs.

2   Cook the edamame (soybeans) in boiling salted water for 3 minutes, then drain and refresh under cold water.

3   Arrange the salad greens, carrot, and tomatoes on small plates, sprinkle with the edamame, and spoon the hummus on top. Sprinkle with the pumpkin seeds and serve. Alternatively, place inside a flatbread and roll up.

{ **Nutritional tip:** Pumpkin seeds are full of zinc and omega-3.

- 216 calories
- 2.9 g saturated fat

Beef salad with green beans & lime marinade

This Asian-inspired salad is crunchy, juicy, and zesty. Poaching the beef in water is healthier than frying it and makes it easier not to overcook. It's also a great way to use the leftovers from a Sunday roast.

Serves 2

3½ oz sirloin, tenderloin, or skirt steak, sliced thinly

1 cup or a handful of trimmed green beans, or 1½ cups snow peas, or a mixture

3½ cups or a handful of spinach leaves

1 cup or a handful of bean sprouts

2 shallots, chopped

a large mixed handful of basil, cilantro, and mint, coarsely chopped

1 tablespoon roasted salted peanuts, roughly chopped

salt

MARINADE

2–3 tablespoons lime juice

1 teaspoon jaggery or brown sugar

1 garlic clove, grated or crushed

2 tablespoons Thai fish sauce

½ hot red Thai chile, chopped

1   First make the marinade by combining all the ingredients in a bowl.

2   Put the beef in a bowl, pour boiling water over it, and let stand for 30 seconds. Drain and return the beef to the bowl, cover with the marinade, and set aside.

3   Cook the beans or snow peas in boiling salted water for 2 minutes. Drain and refresh under cold water. Mix with the spinach, bean sprouts, shallots, and herbs, then combine with the beef and marinade. Sprinkle with the chopped peanuts and serve.

- 172 calories (plus 56 calories if peanuts included)
- 0.6 g saturated fat (plus 0.8 g if peanuts included)

Vietnamese chicken salad itsu

made the mistake of taking this lettuce-free salad off the menu last year. Customer demand made sure of its permanent return two days later. The combination of crunchy vegetables, juicy chicken, and fine noodles in a sweet, hot, salty dressing topped with crunchy peanuts is authentically Vietnamese, and it tastes as good as it looks. If you want to keep the second portion for lunch or dinner the next day, add the dressing just before eating.

Serves 2

½ oz thin cellophane noodles

⅔ cup small, shredded cooked chicken breast pieces

½ shallot, finely sliced

¼ head of napa cabbage or green cabbage, finely sliced

a large handful of bean sprouts

1 carrot, grated or cut into fine sticks

2 mixed handfuls of cilantro, basil, and mint, coarsely chopped

2 tablespoons coarsely chopped peanuts (optional)

1 quantity Sweet Chili Sauce (*see* page 167)

1   Put the noodles in a bowl and cover with boiling water for 3–5 minutes, or according to the package directions. Drain and refresh under cold water, then set aside.

2   Place all the remaining ingredients, apart from the sauce, in a large bowl and mix well. Add the noodles, gently untangling the strands as you work.

3   Pour the sauce over the salad and toss well before serving.

Variation: Try making this with shrimp instead of chicken—a delicious (and still skinny) alternative.

» • 174 calories
• 1.4 g saturated fat

itsu's special salad
Packed with goodness and dressed with our special spicy sauce, this salad is so healthy that you will want to eat it with everything. It keeps well, so can be made in advance, and is perfect as a portable lunch.

Serves 2 as a main course, or 4 as an appetizer

1 oz thin cellophane noodles

⅔ cup edamame (soybeans)

large pinch of dried wakame

2 carrots, grated, or shaved into strips with a potato peeler ....

½ cup mixed chopped cilantro, basil, and mint

1 cup arugula leaves

1 tablespoon pumpkin seeds

2 teaspoons sesame seeds, preferably toasted

3½ oz firm tofu, cut into cubes

2 tablespoons Spicy Sauce (*see* page 171)

Nutritional tips: Carrots are a great source of vitamin A, which is important for a healthy immune system; edamame (soybeans) and tofu both contain high-quality protein and help to maintain a healthy hormone balance.

1   Put the noodles in a bowl and cover with boiling water for 3–5 minutes, or according to the package directions. Drain and refresh under cold water, then set aside.

2   Cook the edamame (soybeans) in boiling water for 3 minutes, then drain and refresh under cold water.

3   Soak the wakame in cold water for 5 minutes, then drain.

4   Put the noodles into a bowl, add the wakame, carrots, herbs, arugula, seeds, tofu, and beans and toss together.

5   Serve the salad with the spicy sauce.

- 87 calories (plus 34 calories if sesame seeds included)
- 0.4 g saturated fat (plus 0.6 g if sesame seeds included)

Crisp salad with sesame dressing

Salads should be fun, easy, and creative, and this colorful mixture of vegetables with creamy sesame sauce fits the bill. It makes a great portable lunch, and is a good way to use up whatever you have in the refrigerator, but try to use ingredients that retain their crunch, such as carrots, radishes, celery, and bell peppers.

Serves 2

3½ cups mixed salad greens

1 carrot, grated or cut into fine sticks

1 red or green bell pepper, cored, seeded, and sliced

1 celery stick, sliced

a small handful of radishes, halved

3 tablespoons Sesame Sauce (*see* page 168)

1 tablespoon sesame seeds, preferably toasted, to serve (optional)

1   Put all the ingredients (apart from the sauce and the seeds) into a bowl. Add the sesame sauce and mix well. Sprinkle with sesame seeds (if using) and serve.

- 151 calories
- 1.4 g saturated fat

Chopped salad with tofu, wakame & miso dressing

Here's a great way to use any vegetables you might have lingering in the refrigerator, such as celery, carrots, and bean sprouts. The creamy dressing turns them into something really special.

Serves 2

½ cucumber, cut into small cubes

a small handful of cherry tomatoes, halved

½ green bell pepper, cored, seeded, and finely chopped

a small handful of radishes, halved

1 scallion, sliced

3½ oz firm tofu, cut into cubes

2 tablespoons dried wakame, soaked in cold water for 5 minutes then drained

1 quantity Miso Dressing (*see* page 168)

1 teaspoon sesame oil

1 tablespoon sesame seeds, preferably toasted, to serve

1 Put all the vegetables into a bowl with the tofu and wakame. Add the dressing and sesame oil and mix gently. Serve with sesame seeds sprinkled over the top.

Tip: At itsu, you'll find wakame in various soups and salads. To prepare it for use, all you need to do is soak the dried leaves in cold water for a few minutes to reconstitute it.

Nutritional tip: Apart from tasting delicious, wakame contains something called fucoxanthin, which can help burn fatty deposits.

- 220 calories
- 2.4 g saturated fat

Carrot & bean salad with toasted seeds
A colorful salad with plenty of crunch, this can be eaten as a small dish, or alongside a main course, such as Broiled Chicken Teriyaki (*see* page 120). If you haven't tried the shallot dressing before, you're in for a treat, and this recipe is a great excuse to make a jar of it to keep in the refrigerator.

Serves 2

1½ cups trimmed green beans

⅔ cup edamame (soybeans)

2 tablespoons mixed pumpkin and sunflower seeds

1 tablespoon soy sauce

2 large or 3 small carrots, shaved into strips with a potato peeler

1–2 tablespoons Shallot Dressing (*see* page 172)

salt

1 Cook the green beans and edamame (soybeans) in boiling salted water for 2 minutes. Drain and refresh under cold water.

2 Heat a dry skillet. Cook the seeds, tossing occasionally, for about 1 minute, or until they start to toast. Pour the soy sauce over the seeds and turn off the heat. It will simmer and evaporate to form a dark, salty coating over the seeds, a little like a peanut brittle.

3 Put the carrots, green beans, and edamame into a bowl and mix well with the dressing. Serve with the toasted seeds sprinkled over the top.

»
- 242 calories
- 1.1 g saturated fat

Soba noodle salad Soft noodles and
crunchy vegetables with a kick of chile make this a filling but healthy salad. It's delicious with sesame seeds sprinkled over at the end.

Serves 2

3 oz soba noodles

¼ cup Sesame Sauce (*see* page 168) ·······················

¾-inch piece of fresh ginger root, grated (about 2 tablespoons)

1 hot red Thai chile, seeded and chopped

a small handful of cilantro, chopped

¼ cucumber, chopped

2 scallions, sliced

1 cup sliced radishes

salt

1 tablespoon sesame seeds, preferably toasted, to serve

Nutritional tip: Tahini (sesame seed paste), a constituent of the sesame sauce, contains vitamin E, an important antioxidant, which protects against cell damage.

1   Cook the soba noodles in 6½ cups of boiling salted water for 7 minutes. Drain and refresh under cold water. Set aside to cool.

2   Put the cold noodles into a bowl, add the sesame sauce and all the remaining ingredients, except for the sesame seeds, and mix well.

3   Divide the salad between 2 plates and sprinkle with the sesame seeds to serve.

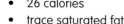

- 26 calories
- trace saturated fat

Pickled cucumber with ginger

This simple, quick pickle tastes great with everything. Try it as a topping for a potsu, with rice or noodles, or added to a salad. It's also good as part of a bento box-style meal, with some Mackerel with Sweet Mirin Sauce (*see* page 154). It's hard to believe that something so tasty is this skinny, plus a portion counts as one of your five-a-day.

Serves 4

2 tablespoons soy sauce

2 tablespoons rice vinegar

1–2 teaspoons sugar or sugar alternative

½ cucumber, peeled and cut in half lengthwise

¾-inch piece of fresh ginger root, thinly sliced

Variations: Other good vegetables to pickle include carrots, fennel, celery, and radishes.

1   Mix together the soy sauce, vinegar, and sugar in a bowl.

2   Using a teaspoon, scrape out and discard the cucumber seeds. Cut the flesh into thin slices.

3   Cut the ginger slices into narrow strips.

4   Add both the cucumber and the ginger to the soy mixture and chill for at least 30 minutes before eating.

- 134 calories
- 1.2 g saturated fat

Spinach balls with sesame sauce

Spinach is a superfood packed with iron, folic acid, and vitamin A. The sesame sauce makes it even more nutritious, being an excellent source of essential fats, magnesium, and calcium.

Serves 2

14 oz spinach (about 13 cups) ....

3 tablespoons Sesame Sauce (*see* page 168)

2 teaspoons sesame seeds, preferably toasted, to serve

Variation: Watercress can be used instead of spinach, and contains even more iron.

1   Cook the spinach in plenty of boiling water for 1–2 minutes, until fully wilted. Drain and refresh under cold water, then use your hands to squeeze it as dry as possible.

2   Divide the spinach in half and shape into two balls. Serve with the sesame sauce poured over the top, and sprinkle with the sesame seeds for extra crunch.

- 101 calories
- 1.4 g saturated fat

Cucumber, sesame & scallion salad

Fresh, light, and bright, this salad is a great addition to all kinds of dishes. Try it with Chicken and Leek Yakitori or Salmon Teriyaki (*see* pages 116 or 136).

Serves 2

½ cucumber, seeded and sliced into sticks

2 small scallions, sliced

2 teaspoons rice vinegar

1 teaspoon mirin

1 tablespoon sesame oil

½ hot red Thai chile, chopped

pinch of salt

1 tablespoon chopped cilantro

1 tablespoon sesame seeds, preferably toasted

1 Arrange the cucumber sticks on a plate and sprinkle the scallion over the top.

2 Combine the vinegar, mirin, sesame oil, chile, and salt and pour the mixture over the cucumber. Sprinkle with the chopped cilantro and sesame seeds before serving.

Nutritional tip: Just a 2-inch piece of cucumber counts as one serving of vegetables.

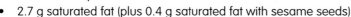

- 275 calories (plus 22 calories with sesame seeds)
- 2.7 g saturated fat (plus 0.4 g saturated fat with sesame seeds)

Baby broccoli with sesame sauce While delicious served warm, this dish can also be eaten cold, perhaps as part of a summer picnic. Sesame sauce is a favorite at itsu and goes wonderfully with all kinds of freshly steamed or boiled leafy greens and beans.

Serves 2

3 cups baby broccoli or broccolini florets

1 quantity Sesame Sauce (*see* page 168)

2 teaspoons sesame seeds, preferably toasted, to serve (optional)

1   Steam the broccoli for 3 minutes, or cook in boiling water for 2 minutes, until just tender. Drain, if necessary, and transfer to a plate.

2   Pour the sesame sauce over the broccoli and sprinkle with sesame seeds (if using) to serve.

Nutritional tip: Gently steaming vegetables preserves more of their nutrients and allows you to get the full benefit of their antioxidants, folic acid, and fiber.

- 63 calories
- 0.6 g saturated fat

Not-too-spicy broccoli

A popular dish served at itsu, this broccoli can also be eaten with your fingers for a healthy, skinny snack or try it as an accompaniment to Seared Miso-Marinated Steak (*see* page 127).

Serves 2

1 (8 oz) package baby broccoli or broccolini

1 teaspoon light oil, such as peanut, for frying

1 hot red Thai chile, seeded and chopped

1 garlic clove, grated or crushed

1½-inch piece of fresh ginger root, grated (about 3 tablespoons)

1 tablespoon soy sauce

flaked salt, to serve

1   Steam the broccoli for 3 minutes, or cook in boiling water for 2 minutes, until just tender. Drain, if necessary, and transfer to a plate.

2   Heat a wok or deep skillet and add the oil. Sauté the chile, garlic, and ginger for 1 minute, stirring well. Add the cooked broccoli and soy sauce and toss to mix.

3   Serve the hot broccoli and sauce with salt flakes sprinkled on top.

- 249 calories
- 4.4 g saturated fat

Tomato, tofu & avocado salad with yuzu-style dressing

This is itsu's dairy-free version of tomato and mozzarella salad—but it's healthier and skinnier than the Italian classic. Serve at room temperature for the best flavor.

Serves 2

1 ripe avocado, pitted, skinned, and sliced

12 sweet cherry tomatoes, halved

2 oz soft/silken tofu, broken into pieces (about ⅓ cup)

2 tablespoons basil and mint leaves

½ quantity Yuzu-style Dressing (*see* page 170)

black pepper

1 Arrange the avocado and tomatoes on a serving plate.

2 Drop the tofu pieces over the top and sprinkle with the herbs and black pepper.

3 Pour the dressing over the salad before serving.

Nutritional tip: Avocados are a rich source of vitamin E, which protects cells from damage.

- 96 calories (plus 34 calories if sesame seeds included)
- 0.4 g saturated fat (plus 0.6 g if sesame seeds included)

Baked eggplant with miso

Miso is a staple in Japanese cooking and an incredibly versatile ingredient in the kitchen. It's now recognized as an umami seasoning—something that adds a depth of flavor to dishes without itself being identifiable. This dish is delicious served hot with rice, or eaten at room temperature the next day.

Serves 2

1 eggplant, cut into ½-inch slices

1 teaspoon light oil, such as peanut, for greasing

small bunch of cilantro, chopped

1 tablespoon sesame seeds, preferably toasted, to sprinkle (optional)

SAUCE

1½ tablespoons miso

2 tablespoons mirin

1 tablespoon sake

¾-inch piece of fresh ginger root, grated (about 2 tablespoons)

2 scallions, sliced

1 Preheat the oven to 400°F.

2 To make the sauce, mix together the miso, mirin, and sake in a large bowl to make a smooth paste. Stir in the ginger and scallions.

3 Add the eggplant slices to the bowl and coat well with the sauce.

4 Grease a roasting pan with the oil and arrange the eggplant slices on it in a single layer so that they cook evenly. Bake for 20 minutes, or until soft and slightly brown. If the eggplant looks a little dry, add a splash of water.

5 Serve sprinkled with the cilantro, plus the sesame seeds if you want some extra crunch.

- 238 calories (plus 34 calories if sesame seeds included; nori negligible)
- 2.2 g saturated fat (plus 0.6 g if sesame seeds included; nori 0 g)

Broiled asparagus with miso hollandaise & poached egg

The Japanese diet contains relatively little dairy produce, but still includes the occasional rich sauce. Miso hollandaise is made without butter, but has all the creamy richness of the French classic. For a more substantial meal, serve the asparagus on a bed of Japanese-style rice as a vegetarian main course.

Serves 2

10½ oz asparagus

2 teaspoons light oil, such as peanut, for drizzling

pinch of salt

2 free-range eggs

1 tablespoon furikake or sesame seeds, preferably toasted, and/or shredded nori, to serve (optional)

1 quantity Miso Hollandaise (*see* page 170)

black pepper

Nutritional tip: Asparagus is packed with even more folic acid than broccoli.

Variation: The dish can be made with other seasonal vegetables, such as baby broccoli or broccolini, carrots, and baby leeks.

1 Heat the broiler to its highest setting.

2 Snap off and discard the woody ends of the asparagus. Lay the asparagus on a baking sheet and drizzle the oil over it. Sprinkle with the salt and toss well to coat.

3 Broil for 8 minutes, checking the spears halfway through the cooking time and giving them a shake so they cook evenly.

4 Poach the eggs in boiling water for 3 minutes so that the white is set but the yolk is still runny.

5 Place the asparagus on serving plates and put an egg on top of each serving. Sprinkle with the seeds and/or nori (if using), season with black pepper, and offer the miso hollandaise alongside.

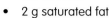

- 189 calories
- 2 g saturated fat

Fried tofu with spicy teriyaki & salad

Warm pieces of tofu coated in a tangy ginger sauce served on a bed of salad make this a skinny but filling dish. It's an excellent vegetarian option, too, because it's full of "good" protein from the tofu.

Serves 1 as a main course or 2 as an appetizer

3½ oz firm tofu, sliced in half

1 teaspoon light oil, such as peanut, for frying

a large handful of mixed salad greens

a large handful of bean sprouts

a small handful of cherry tomatoes, halved

1 tablespoon furikake or sesame seeds, preferably toasted, or pumpkin seeds, or a mixture of all three

DRESSING

2 tablespoons Teriyaki & Ginger Sauce (*see* page 169)

1 teaspoon Sriracha chili sauce

1 tablespoon sesame oil

1   Put the tofu slices on a plate and dab with paper towels to dry.

2   Heat a nonstick skillet until really hot. Add the oil, then sauté the tofu for a minute on each side, until golden brown. Remove from the pan and let cool slightly before cutting into large cubes.

3   Make the dressing by putting all the ingredients into a small bowl and mixing well.

4   Put the salad greens, bean sprouts, and tomatoes on plates and lay the tofu pieces on top. Drizzle with the dressing and sprinkle with the seeds to serve.

Nutritional tip: Bean sprouts contain iron, which is good for the blood. For extra antioxidants, sprinkle the finished dish with pomegranate seeds. (The seeds from half a pomegranate, shared between 2 plates, would add an extra 15 calories per person, but no more saturated fat.)

- 151 calories
- 1 g saturated fat

Spicy hot edamame This is a great
snack to pile into a bowl and share; simply cook the pods whole, then pull
them through your teeth to pop out the little green beans hidden inside.
Steaming instead of boiling the beans locks in maximum nutrients.
A simple bamboo steamer is great for this, but it's not essential.

Serves 2 as an appetizer or 4 as a snack

2 cups edamame (soybeans) in their pods

1 teaspoon light oil, such as peanut, for frying

1 hot red Thai chile, chopped

1 garlic clove, grated or crushed

1½-inch piece of fresh ginger root, finely chopped
(about 3 tablespoons)

1 tablespoon soy sauce

flaked salt, to serve (optional)

1   Steam the edamame (soybean) pods for 3 minutes, or cook them in boiling water
    for 2 minutes. Drain well.

2   Heat a wok or deep skillet and add the oil. Sauté the chile, garlic, and ginger for
    about 1 minute, stirring well. Add the cooked pods and soy sauce and toss to mix.

3   Transfer to a bowl and serve the hot edamame pods and sauce, sprinkled with salt
    flakes, if you desire.

- 274 calories
- 1.1 g saturated fat

Vegetable tempura
Here's a fun and easy way to prepare any seasonal vegetables. The secret to crisp, light tempura batter is to get the oil hot enough and cook only small batches at a time. The hotter the oil, the less it is absorbed by the batter, and the healthier the result. Increase the quantities below and serve the tempura with ponzu sauce for a fabulous party snack. Note that the cooking oil can be reused; just cool and strain it, then store it in an airtight container.

Serves 2

1 small eggplant (about 10 oz)

7 oz asparagus

8 small scallions, trimmed

1 cup trimmed green beans

about 3⅓ cups sunflower oil, for deep-frying

1 quantity Ponzu Sauce (*see* page 169), to serve

BATTER

¾ cup all-purpose flour

3 tablespoons cornstarch

1 teaspoon baking powder

½ teaspoon salt

about 1 cup chilled sparkling water

1. Cut the eggplant in half lengthwise and then slice it into ¼-inch-thick semicircles.

2. Snap off and discard the woody ends of the asparagus. Slice the remainder in half lengthwise and then into short lengths.

3. Cut the scallions into short lengths.

4. To make the batter, sift the flour, cornstarch, and baking powder into a bowl and stir in the salt. Whisk in just under 1 cup of the water to make a smooth batter that has the consistency of heavy cream. Add more water, if necessary.

5. In a deep saucepan, heat the oil to 350°F, or until a teaspoon of batter added to the pan sizzles and starts to brown immediately.

6. Warm a plate and cover it with paper towels.

7. Dip a handful of prepared vegetables into the batter, then carefully lower them one at a time into the hot oil. Cook for less than a minute, until the batter is puffy and golden. Using tongs, transfer them to the prepared plate. Repeat until all the vegetables are cooked.

8. Serve the tempura hot, with the ponzu sauce in a bowl for dipping.

VEGETABLES & SALADS

- 132 calories
- 0.2 g saturated fat

Pickled vegetables with seaweed & edamame

Japanese sea vegetables are treasured ingredients—low in fat and beautifully varied in color, texture, and flavor. You can buy them dried in packages, so they store well and take just a few minutes to prepare. Alternatively, if you can't buy them, just use wakame—you'll still get all those wonderful sea nutrients.

Serves 2

a handful of dried sea vegetables (available online or from good Japanese suppliers—*see* page 188)

⅓ cup edamame (soybeans), fresh or frozen

1 carrot, shaved into thin strips using a potato peeler

1 celery stick, sliced

a small handful of radishes, quartered

1½-inch piece of fresh ginger root, sliced, or 1 tablespoon ready-made pickled ginger

PICKLING SAUCE

3 tablespoons mirin

3 tablespoons rice vinegar

1 teaspoon sugar or sugar alternative

1 teaspoon salt

1   Put the dried sea vegetables into a bowl of warm water and let soak for 10 minutes.

2   Meanwhile, make the pickling sauce. Heat the mirin in a saucepan until it starts to boil. Add the remaining sauce ingredients and cook for 1 minute, until the sugar and salt have dissolved. Pour into a large bowl and let cool.

3   If using fresh edamame (soybeans), cook them for 3 minutes in boiling water; if using frozen, just pour boiling water over them and let stand for 3 minutes. Drain and refresh under cold water.

4   Drain the sea vegetables and add them with all the other vegetables and the ginger to the pickling sauce. Mix well, then cover and refrigerate for up to 24 hours, but for at least 15 minutes.

5   Serve immediately for a fresh crunchy texture, or keep in the refrigerator until needed.

MEAT }

- 182 calories
- 3 g saturated fat

Mini Thai pork burgers These neat little

burgers, which you can eat with your fingers, are great for a picnic, an easy appetizer, or as party snacks. Serve with sweet chili sauce for dipping.

Serves 4

7 oz ground pork

½ lemon grass stalk, finely chopped

2 lime leaves, shredded

½ garlic clove, grated or crushed

¾-inch piece of fresh ginger root, grated (about 2 tablespoons)

1 hot red Thai chile, finely chopped

zest of ½ lime

small bunch of cilantro, chopped, plus extra sprigs to garnish

½ teaspoon salt

1 free-range egg, whisked

flour, for dusting

1 tablespoon light oil, such as peanut, for frying

1 quantity Sweet Chili Sauce (see page 167)

black pepper

1   Put the ground pork into a bowl and add the lemon grass, lime leaves, garlic, ginger, chile, lime zest, cilantro, and salt. Season with black pepper and, using a spoon, or your hands, mix together thoroughly.

2   Pour in half the whisked egg to bring the mixture together, adding the remainder if the mixture seems a little dry.

3   Form the mixture into 12 little balls, then flatten them into patties. Put them on a plate and refrigerate for 10 minutes.

4   Sprinkle some flour on a saucer and season with salt and black pepper. Dust the patties on both sides with the seasoned flour.

5   Heat a large skillet and add the oil. Cook the patties 4–6 at a time, depending on the size of your pan, for 3–4 minutes on each side. Transfer the cooked burgers to a warm plate and cook the remaining patties in the same way.

6   Serve the burgers garnished with cilantro sprigs with the sweet chili sauce for dipping.

- 271 calories (plus 5 calories if sake used in sauce)
- 2.1 g saturated fat

Chicken & leek yakitori

Yakitori means, literally, "skewered chicken." It's really easy to make under the broiler, but even better on a barbecue grill. And kids love it, too! If you're using wooden skewers, remember to soak them in water for about 20 minutes before threading them up so that they don't burn when you grill the skewers. Great served with rice or salad.

Serves 4

14 oz boneless, skinless chicken thighs, cut into cubes ....

3 leeks, cut into 1¼-inch lengths

1 quantity Teriyaki & Ginger Sauce (*see* page 169), plus 1 tablespoon sake (optional)

salt and black pepper

shichimi pepper or dried red pepper flakes, to serve (optional)

Variation: Cherry tomatoes, asparagus, zucchini, or other green vegetables can be used instead of chicken.

1   Heat the broiler to its highest setting.

2   Meanwhile, thread the chicken pieces and leek pieces alternately onto 4 skewers. Sprinkle with a little salt and black pepper and broil for 5–7 minutes on each side.

3   Transfer the chicken skewers to a plate or serving dish and pour or brush the sauce over them. (The sake adds a wonderful flavor, but you can omit it if you don't want the extra calories or are serving the dish to children.)

4   Sprinkle with shichimi pepper or dried red pepper flakes, if using, and serve the skewers immediately.

MEAT

116

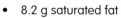

- 257 calories
- 8.2 g saturated fat

Thai green curry with chicken & green beans

A supereasy, skinny, and healthy dinner. Serve with white or brown rice (*see* pages 44 and 45) for a more substantial meal.

Serves 4

1 tablespoon light oil, such as peanut, for frying

14 oz boneless, skinless chicken thighs, cut into bite-size pieces

2 tablespoons Thai green curry paste

2 shallots, finely sliced

1 teaspoon soy sauce

1 teaspoon Thai fish sauce

1 cup coconut milk

2 cups trimmed green beans

2 tablespoons mixed chopped cilantro and basil, to serve

{ **Variation:** Use asparagus, broccoli, or snow peas instead of green beans.

1   Place the oil in a saucepan over high heat. When hot, briefly cook the chicken pieces until they start to brown.

2   Add the curry paste and stir to coat the chicken. Cook for another minute or so, then add the shallots, soy sauce, and fish sauce.

3   Pour in the coconut milk and stir well. Bring to a boil, then simmer for 10 minutes.

4   Add the green beans and a splash of water, if the sauce is looking a little reduced. Cover and cook for another 5 minutes, until the beans soften.

5   Spoon into a serving dish and sprinkle with the herbs to serve.

- 217 calories
- 1.8 g saturated fat

Broiled chicken teriyaki

In this recipe, you can also use breast meat instead of thighs, but make sure you reduce the cooking time slightly. It's delicious served on a bed of *Momofuku*-inspired rice plus some Pickled Cucumber with Ginger on the side (*see* pages 42 and 93).

Serves 2

1 tablespoon light oil, such as peanut, for frying

7 oz boneless, skinless chicken thighs

1 quantity Teriyaki & Ginger Sauce (*see* page 169)

1 tablespoon sesame seeds, preferably toasted, to serve

1   Heat the broiler to its highest setting.

2   Rub a little oil into the chicken and broil for about 5 minutes on each side.

3   Slice the chicken into large pieces and pour the sauce over them. Sprinkle with sesame seeds to serve.

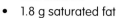

- 256 calories
- 1.8 g saturated fat

Steak teriyaki salad in lettuce cups

There's no need for knives and forks when eating these—just roll the filled lettuce leaves into mini packages and eat using your fingers. Serve these colorful bites as an appetizer, a filling snack, or as canapés with drinks at a party.

Serves 2

2 teaspoons light oil, such as peanut, for frying

3½ oz tenderloin or sirloin steak, cut into bite-size slivers ....

4 iceberg or butterhead lettuce leaves

¼ cucumber, cut into small cubes

a small handful of radishes, thinly sliced lengthwise

½ red onion, thinly sliced

a small handful of cilantro, chopped

1 quantity Teriyaki & Ginger Sauce (*see* page 169)

salt and black pepper

Nutritional tip: Buy smaller amounts of more expensive beef cuts, such as tenderloin, which is low in saturated fat and is a good source of anemia-protective iron.

1   Heat a skillet until really hot. Add the oil, then stir-fry the steak pieces for just a few minutes so that they are still pink inside. Transfer to a plate and season well with salt and black pepper.

2   Put the lettuce leaves on a serving plate and fill with the cucumber, radishes, onion, and cilantro. Season with salt and black pepper. Add the steak pieces, pour the sauce over them, and serve.

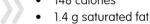

- 148 calories
- 1.4 g saturated fat

Seared beef with celeriac salad

Celeriac, as the name suggests, tastes like celery, but couldn't look more different. It's a knobbly vegetable that is best peeled with a small, sharp knife. Here, it's used in a spicy, crunchy salad to accompany thinly sliced beef, and makes an elegant appetizer.

Serves 2

3½ oz tenderloin or sirlon steak

½ teaspoon light oil, such as peanut, for frying

salt and black pepper

CELERIAC SALAD

2 tablespoons soft/silken tofu

2 tablespoons miso

1½ teaspoons wasabi paste ....

1 teaspoon lemon juice

½ head of celeriac, grated

1 tablespoon mixed chopped chives and parsley

1 Season the beef well on both sides with salt and black pepper.

2 Heat a skillet until really hot. Add the oil, then cook the beef for 2 minutes on each side to get a lovely brown crust. Transfer to a plate to cool.

3 Blend or mix the tofu with the miso, wasabi, and lemon juice to make a smooth paste. Put the celeriac into a bowl with the chives and parsley, then stir in the tofu mixture. Season with black pepper.

4 Slice the beef thinly and arrange on plates with the celeriac salad.

Nutritional tip: Wasabi is antibacterial, detoxifying, and rich in vitamin C. It also aids digestion and is believed to stimulate the appetite.

- 263 calories
- 2.6 g saturated fat

Seared miso-marinated steak

Marinating steak in miso gives it a deep umami flavor. Serve with some Easy Japanese-style Rice (*see* page 44) and Pickled Cucumber with Ginger (*see* page 93) for a healthy meal.

Serves 2

2 tenderloin, sirloin, or skirt steaks, about 5 oz each

MARINADE

2 tablespoons miso

1 tablespoon sake

1 tablespoon mirin

2 teaspoons sugar or sugar alternative

1 tablespoon wasabi paste

1   To make the marinade, mix the miso with the sake in a large bowl to make a smooth paste. Stir in the other ingredients and mix well.

2   Put the steaks in the marinade and turn them over a few times to coat completely. Cover and refrigerate for up to 24 hours, but at least 15 minutes.

3   Heat a large skillet until really hot. Add the oil, then cook the steaks for about 2 minutes on each side—depending on size and how well done you prefer them.

4   Transfer the steaks to a plate, then pour the remaining marinade into the empty pan. Heat for a few seconds so it reduces to a sauce.

5   Slice the steaks thickly, pour the sauce over them, and serve.

FISH }

- 235 calories (with Herb Dressing), 275 calories (with Asian Pesto)
- 2.4 g saturated fat (with Herb Dressing), 3.2 g (with Asian Pesto)

Salmon & tuna tartar

Chopped raw fish with fiery wasabi and a herb dressing is an easy, colorful recipe to serve as an impressive appetizer. It's worth using a good fish dealer to buy the freshest possible fish you can find.

Serves 2

1 teaspoon sesame seeds, preferably toasted

1 teaspoon wasabi paste

1 teaspoon lime juice

1 teaspoon sesame oil

5 oz mixture of skinned salmon and tuna fillet, cut into small pieces

1 quantity Herb Dressing or Asian Pesto (*see* page 166)

baby cress or other small leaves, such as microgreens, to serve

1   Put the sesame seeds, wasabi, lime juice, and oil in a bowl and mix together. Add the fish and carefully fold into the sauce until completely coated.

2   Put a large spoonful of the fish on each plate and pour the dressing or pesto around it. Sprinkle with the baby cress or other small leaves to serve.

- 153 calories
- 1.7 g saturated fat

Seared salmon & new-style sauce

Modern sushi chefs sear the outside of fish for added depth of flavor. They use a blowtorch, but it's also easy to do this in a really hot, nonstick skillet. You can serve this dish as sliced sashimi for an appetizer, or keep the salmon pieces whole and serve two as a main course with itsu's Special Salad (*see* page 84).

Serves 4 as a small plate

1 teaspoon light oil, such as peanut, for frying

7 oz skinned salmon fillet ....

1 quantity New-Style Sauce (*see* page 167)

Tip: Before searing fish, dry it well with paper towels—this helps to prevent it from sticking to the pan.

TO SERVE

2 chives, cut into 4-inch lengths

1 slice of fresh ginger root, 4 inches long, cut into fine strips

sesame seeds, preferably toasted

1   Heat a nonstick skillet until really hot. Add the oil, then sear the salmon for about 1 minute on each side, until the outside is golden brown but the center remains pink. Transfer to a plate to cool.

2   When ready to serve, cut the salmon into thin slices and arrange on serving plates.

3   Pour the sauce over the fish, garnish with the chives and ginger, then sprinkle with sesame seeds.

- 296 calories
- 2.8 g saturated fat

Pan-fried salmon & wasabi peas

Thanks to Nicola Formby for this one. Nicola worked tirelessly with itsu over the years to help develop recipes and delicious sauces, and this dish is consistently one of her best sellers. Bravo! At itsu, we serve it as sashimi (*see* page 13), but it is also great as a main course.

Serves 2

1 teaspoon light oil, such as peanut, for frying

2 skinned salmon fillets, about 3½ oz each

½ quantity New-Style Sauce (*see* page 167)

pea shoots, to garnish (optional)

PEAS

1 cup fresh or frozen small peas

2 tablespoons Spicy Sauce (*see* page 171)

1 teaspoon wasabi paste

large pinch of salt

½ teaspoon black pepper

1 First cook the peas in boiling salted water for 2 minutes, then drain. Transfer them to a bowl and mix in the spicy sauce, wasabi, salt, and black pepper. Mash or blend the mixture for just a few seconds to lightly crush the peas. Set aside.

2 Heat a nonstick skillet until really hot. Add the oil, then sear the salmon for about 1 minute on each side, until the outside is golden brown but the center remains pink. Transfer to a plate to cool.

3 To serve, spoon the peas onto plates and place the salmon fillets on top. Pour a little of the new-style sauce over each serving and offer the rest separately. Garnish with pea shoots, if you desire.

Nutritional tip: Peas are a great source of iron and fiber, including soluble fiber, which is good for regulating cholesterol.

Variation: Edamame (soybeans) or fava beans can be used instead of peas. Cook them in exactly the same way.

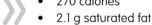

- 270 calories
- 2.1 g saturated fat

Salmon teriyaki We like to cook our salmon

so that it's served a little rare inside, which means it's juicier. Serve this delicious salmon on a bed of Japanese-style Rice with Scallion & Ginger Sauce or with itsu's Special Salad (*see* pages 42 or 84) with the sticky sauce drizzled over the top.

Serves 2

1 quantity Teriyaki & Ginger Sauce (*see* page 169)

1 teaspoon light oil, such as peanut, for frying

2 skinned salmon fillets, about 3½ oz each ....

> **Nutritional tip:** Salmon is a great source of omega-3, and if you buy wild salmon, it contains less fat than the farmed type.

1 Gently warm the sauce in a small saucepan.

2 Heat a nonstick skillet until really hot, add the oil, then cook the salmon fillets for 2–4 minutes on each side, depending on their thickness, until the outside is brown and crisp while the inside remains a little pink.

3 Serve the salmon on a bed of rice or salad with the sauce poured over the top.

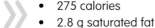

- 275 calories
- 2.8 g saturated fat

Seared tuna with sesame & spicy sauce

Tuna and sesame seeds are made for each other. This superhealthy, easy main course is made extraspecial with itsu's spicy sauce. It's great with peppery salad greens, such as arugula or mizuna, dressed with a drizzle of plain sesame oil or Yuzu-style Dressing (*see* page 170).

Serves 2

2 tuna steaks, about 4½ oz each ....

1 tablespoon soy sauce

1 teaspoon light oil, such as peanut, for frying

TO SERVE

1 tablespoon sesame seeds, preferably toasted

1 teaspoon chopped chives

peppery salad greens

2–3 tablespoons Spicy Sauce (*see* page 171)

Nutritional tips: Tuna is packed with omega-3s for a healthy heart and brain, while sesame seeds contain loads of magnesium, a mineral that is important for energy levels and a healthy nervous system. The seeds are also great for topping up levels of calcium, iron, zinc, and essential fats.

1   Put the tuna steaks on a plate and pour the soy sauce over them. Turn to cover them completely in the sauce.

2   Heat a skillet until really hot. Add the oil, then cook the tuna steaks for about 1 minute on each side so that the middle remains a little pink.

3   Serve each steak sprinkled with the sesame seeds and chives, and accompanied by peppery salad greens, with the sauce offered alongside.

FISH

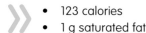

- 123 calories
- 1 g saturated fat

Hot shrimp with no-mayo mayonnaise

A beautiful pile of pink shrimp on a bed of green spinach and arugula, this is a beautiful light meal, and it is great as a sharing plate, too—just put it in the middle of the table for everyone to dip into.

Serves 2

3½ oz uncooked peeled shrimp, tails left on

1 tablespoon light oil, such as peanut, for frying

large pinch of salt

2 handfuls of mixed baby spinach and arugula leaves

1 quantity Sweet Citrus No-Mayo Mayonnaise (*see* page 172)

chopped chives, to garnish

1   Rinse the shrimp and dry well using a piece of paper towel.

2   Heat a skillet or wok until really hot, then add the oil. Add the shrimp and stir-fry for 2–3 minutes, until they start to color, then sprinkle with the salt.

3   To serve, place a pile of leaves on each plate and arrange the shrimp alongside, sprinkled with the chives. Serve with a bowl of the "mayo" on the side for dipping.

Variation: For a vegetarian alternative, use fried tofu instead of shrimp.

Nutritional tip: Spinach is a great source of lutine, which protects the health of your eyes.

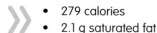

- 279 calories
- 2.1 g saturated fat

Spicy shrimp cocktail Fresh, spicy shrimp piled
on a healthy, crunchy salad—this is seriously delicious yet light and full of goodness.

Serves 2 as a main course

5 oz cooked peeled shrimp,
tails discarded

2 tablespoons Spicy Sauce
(*see* page 171)

2 handfuls of mixed salad greens

2 teaspoons sesame oil

CELERIAC SALAD

2 tablespoons soft/silken tofu

2 tablespoons miso

1½ teaspoons wasabi paste

½ head of celeriac, grated

1 tablespoon mixed chopped chives
and parsley

1   Put the shrimp into a bowl and stir in the spicy sauce. Set aside.

2   Blend or mix the tofu with the miso and wasabi to make a smooth paste. Put the celeriac in a bowl with the chives and parsley and stir in the tofu mixture.

3   To serve, dress the salad greens with the sesame oil and place some on each plate. Add a spoonful of the celeriac salad and place the spicy shrimp on top.

Variation: Use Sweet Citrus No-Mayo Mayonnaise (*see* page 172) instead of the Spicy Sauce.

- 99 calories
- 2.4 g saturated fat

Jumbo shrimp with crisp garlic & chile

You can serve these spicy tidbits straight from the pan, dipping them in a Japanese-style no-mayo lemon, lime, and orange sauce and eating them with your fingers. Alternatively, make them part of a simple summer lunch.

Serves 2

1 teaspoon light oil, such as peanut, for frying

14 oz uncooked jumbo shrimp in their shells, tails left on
(about 2 per person)

1 garlic clove, finely sliced

1 hot red Thai chile, finely chopped

splash of soy sauce

1 quantity Sweet Citrus No-Mayo Mayonnaise (*see* page 172)

lemon wedges, to serve

1   Heat a skillet or wok until really hot, then add the oil. Add the shrimp and cook for at least 1 minute on each side, until crisp and slightly brown. Transfer to a plate.

2   Add the garlic and chile to the pan and cook for a few seconds, until starting to brown. Return the shrimp to the pan, add a splash of soy sauce, and toss together.

3   Serve with a bowl of sweet citrus mayonnaise and wedges of lemon on the side.

- 274 calories (plus 17 calories with the dipping sauce)
- 0.9 g saturated fat (no extra fat with the dipping sauce)

Jumbo shrimp tempura

Fat, juicy jumbo shrimp in the lightest possible batter are delicious, especially if dipped in a zesty sauce. They are quick to make and also great to serve as finger food at parties. Note that the cooking oil can be reused; just cool and strain it, then store it in an airtight container.

Serves 2

7 oz uncooked peeled jumbo shrimp with tails left on

about 3⅓ cups sunflower oil, for deep-frying

1 quantity Ponzu Sauce (*see* page 169)

BATTER

¾ cup all-purpose flour

3 tablespoons cornstarch

1 teaspoon baking powder

½ teaspoon salt

about 1 cup chilled sparkling water

Variation: For something really special, try these shrimp as a filling in hand rolls (*see* page 62). Just don't forget to first remove their tails!

1   Sift the flour, cornstarch, and baking powder into a bowl, then stir in the salt. Whisk in just under 1 cup of the water to make a smooth batter that has the consistency of pouring cream. Add more water, if necessary.

2   Put the raw shrimp on a plate next to the bowl of batter. Place a piece of paper towel on another plate.

3   In a deep saucepan or wok, heat the oil to 350°F or until a teaspoon of batter sizzles and starts to brown immediately.

4   Dip the shrimp into the batter, then carefully lower them one at a time into the hot oil. Cook for about 1 minute, until the batter is puffy and golden, then, using tongs, transfer them to the prepared plate. Cook the rest of the shrimp in the same way.

5   Serve hot, offering the ponzu sauce in a bowl for dipping.

- 128 calories
- 0.9 g saturated fat

Spicy squid salad
Delicious hot or cold, this salad is great for an easy appetizer and can be made in advance.

Serves 4

2 teaspoons light oil, such as peanut, for frying

2 shallots, sliced

2 lime leaves, finely chopped

1 lemon grass stalk, finely chopped

1 hot red Thai chile, finely chopped

7 oz baby squid with tentacles, cleaned ....

juice of 1 lime

2 tablespoons mixed chopped cilantro, basil, and mint

1 cup bean sprouts

2 handfuls of mixed salad greens

1 tablespoon sesame oil

1 quantity Sweet Chili Sauce (*see* page 167)

Nutritional tip: Just one serving of squid provides your daily requirement of the important antioxidant selenium.

1   Heat a skillet, add the oil, then add the shallots, lime leaves, lemon grass, and chile. Cook for 2 minutes, until the shallots start to soften and color slightly.

2   Add the squid and stir-fry over high heat for just a minute or so, until the flesh turns white—any longer and it will become tough.

3   Pour the lime juice over the squid and toss again before removing from the heat.

4   Put the herbs, bean sprouts, and salad greens into a bowl, drizzle with the sesame oil, and toss to coat.

5   To serve, put a small pile of the salad mixture on each plate, arrange the squid on top or alongside, and pour a spoonful of sweet chili sauce over each serving.

- 247 calories
- 2.3 g saturated fat

Crispy chile squid
At itsu, we use karaage flour (potato starch) to give our squid a really crisp coating, but all-purpose flour mixed half-and-half with cornstarch is a great substitute. Try adding shichimi pepper to the flour if you like your food to have a fiery kick.

Serves 2

⅓ cup all-purpose flour

⅓ cup cornstarch

large pinch of salt

1 teaspoon shichimi pepper (optional)

7 oz baby squid with tentacles, cleaned and sliced into rings

about 2½ cups sunflower oil, for deep-frying

TO SERVE

1 red chile, sliced

1 quantity Sweet Chili Sauce (see page 167)

1   Combine the flour and cornstarch in a bowl and add the salt and shichimi pepper (if using). Toss the squid in the flour.

2   In a deep saucepan or wok, heat the oil to 350°F, or until a piece of floured squid sizzles and starts to brown immediately.

3   Carefully add a handful of squid at a time to the hot oil. Cook for just 1 minute—any longer and it will become tough—then drain on paper towels while you cook the next batch.

4   To serve, sprinkle the chile over the squid and offer the sauce in a small bowl for dipping.

- 117 calories
- 0.6 g saturated fat

Scallop salad with chile, scallions & crisp garlic

Ideal for a quick dinner or an elegant appetizer, these scallops can be served hot or cold, so it's a great dish to prepare ahead of time.

Serves 2

2 teaspoons light oil, such as peanut, for frying

1 garlic clove, finely sliced

3½ oz scallops (2 large or 3 medium per person) ....

1 hot red Thai chile, finely sliced

1 large scallion, sliced

1 tablespoon soy sauce

2 handfuls of arugula or mixed peppery salad greens

2 handfuls of bean sprouts

1 tablespoon Yuzu-style Dressing (*see* page 170)

Nutritional tip: Scallops are a source of zinc, which helps maintain a healthy immune system.

1. Heat a skillet or wok until really hot. Add the oil, then stir-fry the garlic for a few seconds, until golden. Transfer to a plate, making sure you get everything out so there is nothing left to burn.

2. Add the scallops to the pan and cook for just 1–2 minutes on each side.

3. Add the chile and scallion and cook for another minute to soften slightly. Pour in the soy sauce, give it a quick stir, and remove from the heat.

4. Mix the leaves and bean sprouts in a bowl with the dressing. Toss well and divide between 2 plates. Place 2 or 3 scallops alongside each pile of leaves, add some of the scallion and chile, and sprinkle the crisp garlic over the top.

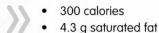

- 300 calories
- 4.3 g saturated fat

Mackerel with sweet mirin sauce

Fresh mackerel is unbelievably good for you because it contains the highest amount of omega-3 fatty acids in any fish. The sweet sauce used here makes the ideal accompaniment to its rich, oily flavor. This is great served with rice and Pickled Cucumber with Ginger (*see* page 93).

Serves 2

2 teaspoons sake

2 teaspoons mirin

1 tablespoon soy sauce

¾-inch piece of fresh ginger root, grated (about 2 tablespoons)

1 teaspoon light oil, such as peanut, for frying

2 fresh mackerel fillets, skin on

1   Mix the sake, mirin, soy sauce, and ginger in a small bowl. Set aside.

2   Heat a nonstick skillet, add the oil, and cook the mackerel for about 2 minutes on each side, until the skin is crisp and the flesh is lightly browned. Pour the sauce into the pan and turn off the heat. It will sizzle and reduce slightly and coat the fish.

3   Cut each fillet in half. Serve on a bed of rice with pickled cucumber with ginger, if you desire.

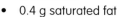

- 110 calories
- 0.4 g saturated fat

Baked sea bass with ginger & scallion

Steaming the fish in little foil pouches makes this an easy, mess-free meal. The other ingredients all steep into the fish to give it a fragrant, delicious flavor. Serve with Spinach Balls with Sesame Sauce (*see* page 94) for the perfect easy dinner.

Serves 2

2 skinned sea bass fillets, about
3½ oz each

2 scallions, sliced

½-inch piece of fresh ginger root, sliced

2 tablespoons soy sauce

black pepper

steamed bok choy or other vegetables,
to serve

1   Preheat the oven to 400°F.

2   Cut two 8½ x 11-inch sheets of aluminum foil and lay a sea bass fillet on each one. Sprinkle with the scallions, ginger, and black pepper, then fold up the foil, scrunching the edges together, but leaving a small gap in the top of each package. Pour the soy sauce into the gap, then seal the packages completely.

3   Bake for 8–10 minutes, then carefully unwrap the packages and transfer the fish to plates, pouring the sauce over the top. Serve with your chosen vegetables.

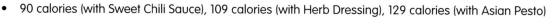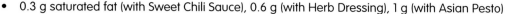

- 90 calories (with Sweet Chili Sauce), 109 calories (with Herb Dressing), 129 calories (with Asian Pesto)
- 0.3 g saturated fat (with Sweet Chili Sauce), 0.6 g (with Herb Dressing), 1 g (with Asian Pesto)

Crab crystal rolls
Once you realize how surprisingly easy these rolls are to make, you can play around with the ingredients, perhaps adding green beans instead of asparagus, or trying different leaves and herbs.

Serves 4

3½ oz cooked crabmeat

2 teaspoons lemon juice

½ oz thin cellophane noodles

4 asparagus spears

4 outer leaves of butterhead lettuce

1 teaspoon chopped chives

2 tablespoons cilantro leaves

4 spring roll wrappers

salt and black pepper

dipping sauce, such as Sweet Chili Sauce, Herb Dressing, or Asian Pesto (*see* pages 166–67)

1 Put the crabmeat into a bowl and add the lemon juice and some black pepper. Stir to combine, then set aside.

2 Put the noodles into a large heatproof bowl and cover them with boiling water. Leave for 3 minutes (or as per the package directions), then drain and refresh under cold water.

3 Cook the asparagus in boiling salted water for 3 minutes, then drain and refresh. Cut in half lengthwise.

4 Cut the stems off the lettuce leaves and tear the leaves in half.

5 Place all the prepared ingredients, together with the herbs, around a clean board. Fill a large bowl with boiling water.

6 Dampen the board slightly where you will prepare the rolls, then dip a wrapper into the boiling water, turning it until wet all over. Don't let it stay in the water too long—when finished, it should still feel a little firm. Lay the sheet flat on the damp board, trying to avoid creasing it.

7 Arrange a tablespoon of crabmeat in a strip on the wrapper, just above the center, leaving a 1-inch gap at each end. Sprinkle with one-quarter of the herbs, then place 2 halved lettuce leaves on top. Add a layer of cooked noodles, and finally 2 slices of asparagus.

8 Lift the top edge of the wrapper, bring it down over the layered filling, and tuck it underneath. Now roll it toward you, folding in the sides as you work so that they are sealed inside the roll. The sheet will stick to itself, leaving you with one long roll, sealed at both ends. Cut it in half diagonallly and set aside while you make the other rolls.

9 Arrange the halved rolls on a serving plate with a bowl of the dipping sauce in the middle, or serve 2 halves per person, offering the sauce separately.

- 66 calories
- 1 g saturated fat

Shrimp crystal rolls
At itsu, we make these rolls twice a day, not only because they are quick and easy, but so that they also taste their freshest. These thin spring roll wrappers (available from most big supermarkets and Asian food stores) have a beautiful translucent quality when wet.

Serves 4

4 spring roll wrappers

½ avocado, pitted, skinned, and thinly sliced

1 carrot, shaved into strips using a potato peeler

¼ cucumber, seeded and cut into strips

a few leaves of butterhead, romaine, or iceberg lettuce, stems removed

2 oz cooked peeled shrimp, tails discarded

4 teaspoons Asian Pesto or Herb Dressing (see page 166)

4 pinches of shichimi pepper or dried red pepper flakes

1 quantity Sweet Chili Sauce (see page 167), or any other favorite dipping sauce, to serve

1   Place all the ingredients around a clean board. Fill a large bowl with boiling water.

2   Dampen the board slightly where you will prepare the rolls, then dip a wrapper into the boiling water, turning it until wet all over. Don't let it stay in the water too long—when finished, it should still feel a little firm. Lay the sheet flat on the damp board, trying to avoid creasing it.

3   Lay a few slices of avocado along the wrapper, just above the center, leaving a 1-inch gap at each end. Add a few strips of the carrot and cucumber, then a few torn strips of lettuce.

4   Take about 1 tablespoon of the shrimp and sprinkle it along the lettuce. Pour a teaspoon of the Asian pesto or herb dressing over the top and add a good pinch of shichimi pepper or dried red pepper flakes.

5   Lift the top edge of the wrapper over the layered filling and tuck it underneath. Now roll it toward you, folding in the sides as you work so that they are sealed inside the roll. The sheet will stick to itself, leaving you with one long roll, sealed at both ends. Cut it in half diagonallly and set aside while you make the other rolls.

6   Serve 2 halves per person, offering the sweet chili sauce separately for dipping.

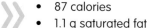

- 87 calories
- 1.1 g saturated fat

Spicy tuna crystal rolls
Fresh tuna is absolutely delicious in these rolls, but very fresh salmon fillet or our cooked tangy tuna mix (*see* page 79) are great alternatives. Choose your favorite dipping sauce, to serve.

Serves 4

3½ oz very fresh tuna, chopped

¼ cup Spicy Sauce (*see* page 171)

4 outer leaves of butterhead, romaine, or iceberg lettuce, firm stems removed

½ carrot, shaved into strips using a potato peeler

¼ avocado, pitted, skinned, and thinly sliced

1 teaspoon chopped chives

4 spring roll wrappers

1 quantity Sweet Chili Sauce (*see* page 167), or any other favorite dipping sauce, to serve

1 Put the chopped tuna into a bowl and mix in the spicy sauce.

2 Place all the remaining ingredients around a clean board. Fill a large bowl with boiling water.

3 Dampen the board slightly where you will prepare the rolls, then dip a wrapper into the boiling water, turning it until wet all over. Don't let it stay in the water too long—when finished, it should still feel a little firm. Lay the sheet flat on the damp board, trying to avoid creasing it.

4 Lay one-quarter of the tuna in a long strip on the wrapper, just above the center, leaving a 1-inch gap at each end. Tear a lettuce leaf in half and place it over the tuna. Add some carrot and avocado strips as the next layer, then sprinkle with the chives.

5 Lift the top edge of the wrapper over the layered filling and tuck it underneath. Now roll it toward you, folding in the sides as you work so that they are sealed inside the roll. The sheet will stick to itself, leaving you with one long roll, sealed at both ends. Cut it in half diagonallly and set aside while you make the other rolls.

6 Serve 2 halves per person, offering your choice of sauce separately for dipping.

DRESSINGS & SAUCES

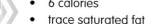

- 6 calories
- trace saturated fat

Homemade dashi stock

Dashi, a simple stock, is a particularly important ingredient in Japanese cooking because it forms the flavor base for most soups. Unlike French stocks, which take hours to make, dashi is quick and easy to put together because you need only two ingredients plus water. Kombu and bonito flakes are readily available from Japanese suppliers (*see* page 188). Stored in an airtight container, the dashi will keep for up to three days in the refrigerator, or it can be frozen.

Serves 2 (makes about 3⅓ cups)

2 large pieces of kombu

4¼ cups water

1½ cups bonito flakes

1   Wipe the kombu with a damp cloth, then place in a saucepan with the water and let soften for about 30 minutes.

2   When the kombu is soft, place the pan over the heat and bring almost to a boil. Take off the heat and discard the kombu.

3   Add the bonito flakes to the hot water and let steep (off the heat) for 10 minutes.

4   Strain the liquid into a clean container, discarding the bonito flakes.

5   Use the stock immediately, or store as recommended above until needed.

- 63 calories
- 0.8 g saturated fat

Asian pesto

Here's a herb-filled, fresh dressing to add some zing to your salads or crystal rolls. You can also use it in recipes as an alternative to Herb Dressing (*see* right). Stored in a screw-top jar, it will keep for up to a week in the refrigerator.

Serves 4

large bunch of cilantro

a few sprigs of mint

2 scallions

1 hot red Thai chile, seeded

1 tablespoon prepared pickled ginger or grated fresh ginger root

1 garlic clove, grated or crushed

2 tablespoons sesame oil

1 tablespoon soy sauce

1 tablespoon lemon juice

1 teaspoon sugar or sugar alternative

½ teaspoon salt

1   Put all the ingredients into a blender and blend to a smooth sauce with flecks of herbs. Or chop the herbs, scallions, chile, and ginger as finely as possible by hand. Put into a bowl, add the remaining ingredients, and mix well.

2   Use the sauce immediately, or store in a screw-top jar in the refrigerator until needed.

- 43 calories
- 0.4 g saturated fat

Herb dressing

This vibrant green, creamy dressing can be used on all kinds of dishes, such as Salmon & Tuna Tartar (*see* page 131). It's great as a salad dressing or a dipping sauce. Stored in a screw-top jar, it will keep for up to a week in the refrigerator.

Serves 4

large bunch of cilantro

1 tablespoon soft/silken tofu

2 lime leaves

1 teaspoon grated fresh ginger root

1 tablespoon brown sugar or sugar alternative

1 teaspoon rice vinegar

1 teaspoon Thai fish sauce

1 teaspoon lime juice

1 tablespoon sesame oil

1   To achieve the best consistency, put all the ingredients into a blender and blend to make a smooth sauce.

2   Use immediately, or store in a screw-top jar in the refrigerator until needed.

DRESSINGS & SAUCES

- 48 calories
- 0.2 g saturated fat

- 77 calories
- 0.8 g saturated fat

Sweet chili sauce

This fresh and punchy dipping sauce goes with loads of dishes, such as crystal rolls, chile squid, and mini pork burgers. It can also be used as a dressing for spicy salads. Stored in a screw-top jar, the sauce will keep for up to two weeks in the refrigerator.

Serves 2

2 tablespoons Thai fish sauce

1 tablespoon jaggery, brown sugar, or sugar alternative

1 tablespoon rice vinegar

1 teaspoon lime juice

1 teaspoon lemon juice

½ teaspoon grated fresh ginger root

½ hot red Thai chile, finely chopped

1 teaspoon sesame oil

1   Put the fish sauce into a bowl, add the sugar, and stir until dissolved. Add the remaining ingredients and stir again.

2   Use the sauce immediately, or store in a screw-top jar in the refrigerator until needed.

New-style sauce

Both salty and zingy, this is a great dressing for sesame-coated broiled salmon or pan-fried mackerel. Stored in a screw-top jar, it will keep for up to two weeks in the refrigerator.

Serves 2

1 garlic clove, grated or crushed

¼ cup soy sauce

¾-inch piece of fresh ginger root, grated (about 2 tablespoons)

1 teaspoon lemon juice

2 teaspoons mirin

1 tablespoon sesame oil

1   Put all the ingredients into a bowl and stir well.

2   Use the sauce immediately, or store in a screw-top jar in the refrigerator until needed.

- 43 calories
- 0 g saturated fat

Miso dressing

A great dressing on vegetables, salads, and even rice. We use sweet miso, which is paler and less salty than other types, but try experimenting with red (dark) miso, too. Stored in a screw-top jar, it will keep for up to two weeks in the refrigerator.

Serves 2

2 tablespoons miso paste

1 tablespoon mirin

2 teaspoons rice vinegar

1 teaspoon lemon juice

1 tablespoon water

black pepper

1   Put the miso into a bowl, add the mirin, and mix to make a smooth paste. Add the remaining ingredients and stir well.

2   Use the dressing immediately, or store in a screw-top jar in the refrigerator until needed.

- 121 calories
- 1.3 g saturated fat

Sesame sauce

A favorite at itsu, this creamy, nutty sauce is served with baby broccoli (broccolini) or steamed spinach, but it could also be used as a dressing for soba noodles, as a dip for crudités, or spooned over broiled tuna or chicken. Stored in a screw-top jar, the sauce will keep for up to two weeks in the refrigerator.

Serves 4

¼ cup mirin

3 tablespoons tahini paste

1 tablespoon soy sauce

3 tablespoons lemon juice

1 teaspoon sesame oil

1 teaspoon sugar or sugar alternative

1 small garlic clove, grated or crushed

1 tablespoon water

1   Put all the ingredients into a bowl and stir well to make a smooth sauce.

2   Use the sauce immediately, or store in a screw-top jar in the refrigerator until needed.

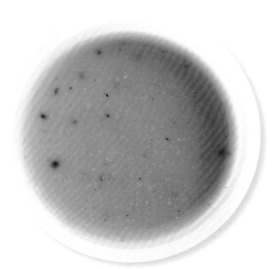

- 86 calories
- 0 g saturated fat

Teriyaki & ginger sauce

This supertasty sauce can be used in many different ways—on broiled chicken, salmon, or steak; poured over rice; or to dress salads. Sweet yet salty, it is full of goodness. Stored in a screw-top jar, it will keep for up to two weeks in the refrigerator. If the sauce thickens during storage, loosen it with water before use.

Serves 2

3 tablespoons mirin

3 tablespoons soy sauce

1 tablespoon sugar or sugar alternative

2 teaspoons rice vinegar

1 teaspoon cornstarch

1½-inch piece of fresh ginger root, grated (about 3 tablespoons)

1   Put all the ingredients into a small saucepan and stir well. Bring to a boil and simmer for a couple of minutes, stirring constantly, to reduce and form a thick syrup.

2   Use the sauce immediately, or store in a screw-top jar in the refrigerator until needed.

Nutritional tip: Ginger contains anti-inflammatory components, and some people swear it helps ease their joints. It's also a good stomach soother.

- 17 calories
- 0 g saturated fat

Ponzu sauce

This is a great citrus-flavored, salty sauce for dipping tempura or sashimi. Stored in a screw-top jar, it will keep for up to two weeks in the refrigerator.

Serves 2

¼ cup soy sauce

4 teaspoons mirin

1 tablespoon orange or mandarin juice

1 teaspoon lemon or lime juice

1   Put all the ingredients into a blender and blend to make a smooth sauce.

2   Use the sauce immediately, or store in a screw-top jar in the refrigerator until needed.

Variation: If you can find bottled yuzu juice, use 4 teaspoons of it instead of the other fruit juices.

- 90 calories
- 0 g saturated fat

- 35 calories
- 0.4 g saturated fat

Miso hollandaise

Despite containing no butter or eggs—major constituents of traditional hollandaise—this version has all the creamy richness you'd hope for. Serve it with broiled asparagus, or on new potatoes or other lightly steamed seasonal vegetables. Stored in a screw-top jar, it will keep for up to two weeks in the refrigerator.

Serves 2 with a main course

¼ cup soft/silken tofu

2 teaspoons soy sauce

¼ cup miso paste

2 teaspoons rice vinegar

1 tablespoon lemon juice

black pepper

1   Put all the ingredients into a bowl or blender and blend to make a smooth sauce.

2   Use immediately, or store in a screw-top jar in the refrigerator until needed.

Yuzu-style dressing

Pimp up your salad greens with this easy citrus-flavored dressing. The Japanese fruit called "yuzu" looks like a small, knobbly grapefruit and tastes tart but sweet. You can buy yuzu juice from specialty Japanese suppliers (*see* page 188), but the combination of juices listed below makes a delicious alternative. Stored in a screw-top jar, the dressing will keep for up to two weeks in the refrigerator.

Serves 4

1 tablespoon soy sauce

1 tablespoon mandarin or orange juice

1 teaspoon lime juice

1 teaspoon lemon juice

2 tablespoons sesame oil or other light oil

black pepper

1   Put all the ingredients into a small bowl and whisk well.

2   Use immediately, or store in a screw-top jar in the refrigerator until needed.

Nutritional tip: Full of vitamin C from the citrus juices and made with no added salt, this dressing is a really healthy option.

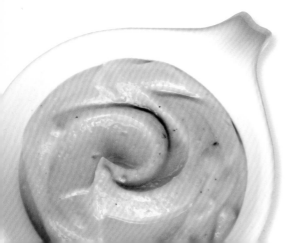

- 64 calories
- 0.7 g saturated fat

Spicy sauce At itsu,

you'll find this spicy sauce everywhere that mayo usually appears. It contains 74 percent less fat than mayo and tastes ten times as good. Use it on seared salmon sashimi, as well as on smoked chicken, shrimp, and even in sushi. Stored in a screw-top jar, it will keep for up to two weeks in the refrigerator. If the sauce thickens slightly during storage, loosen it with a little lemon juice or water before use.

Serves 6

½ cup soft/silken tofu

1 tablespoon tahini paste

1 tablespoon Sriracha chili sauce
or 1 hot red Thai chile, chopped

2 tablespoons lemon juice

1 tablespoon sugar or sugar alternative

¾-inch piece of fresh ginger root, grated
(about 2 tablespoons)

2 garlic cloves, grated or crushed

1½ teaspoons black pepper

½ teaspoon salt

1 tablespoon water

1 tablespoon light oil, such as peanut or grapeseed

1   Put all the ingredients into a blender and blend to make a smooth sauce.

2   Use the sauce immediately, or store in a screw-top jar in the refrigerator until needed.

- 122 calories
- 0.9 g saturated fat

Toasted pumpkin seed topping These seeds

make a great salty, crunchy topping for potsus or salads, and they are also delicious as a healthy snack. Stored in a screw-top jar, they will keep for up to two weeks in a pantry.

Serves 2

3½ tablespoons pumpkin seeds

2 tablespoons soy sauce

1   Heat a dry skillet. When hot, add the pumpkin seeds and toast for just 1 minute, tossing occasionally, until they start to crackle and brown.

2   Turn off the heat and pour in the soy sauce, which will bubble dramatically and then settle.

3   Scrape the mixture into a bowl and eat piping hot, or let cool and store in a screw-top jar until needed.

- 44 calories
- 1.3 g saturated fat

- 43 calories
- 0.5 g saturated fat

Shallot dressing
Sweet, caramelized shallots with a peppery wasabi kick, this is a delicious dressing for salads, and it is also great served with broiled chicken or steak. Stored in a screw-top jar, it will keep for up to two weeks in the refrigerator.

Serves 4

1 tablespoon light oil, such as peanut, for frying

2–3 small shallots, minced (you can do this with an immersion blender)

1 tablespoon water

2 teaspoons sugar or sugar alternative

3 tablespoons soy sauce

2 tablespoons rice wine vinegar

¾-inch piece of fresh ginger root, grated (about 2 tablespoons)

1 teaspoon black pepper

½ teaspoon wasabi powder or 1 teaspoon wasabi paste

1 tablespoon sesame oil

1   Heat the oil in a small saucepan. Add the shallots, water, and sugar, then cover and cook over low heat for 10 minutes.

2   Meanwhile, mix all the remaining ingredients, except the sesame oil, in a bowl.

3   When the shallots are soft, sweet, and a little brown, add them to the soy mixture. Pour in the sesame oil and stir well.

4   Use the sauce immediately, or store in a screw-top jar in the refrigerator until needed.

Sweet citrus no-mayo mayonnaise
At itsu we never use mayo. Once you've tried this alternative, you won't either! It's not only a delicious dip for crisp-fried shrimp or tempura, but it also makes a great salad dressing. Stored in a screw-top jar, it will keep for up to two weeks in the refrigerator.

Serves 4

¼ cup soft/silken tofu

1 tablespoon sesame oil

1 tablespoon mandarin or orange juice

1 teaspoon lemon juice

1 teaspoon lime juice

1 teaspoon soy sauce

½ teaspoon wasabi paste

1 small shallot, grated or finely chopped

1 tablespoon prepared pickled ginger, finely chopped

1   For the best texture, put all the ingredients into a blender and blend until smooth.

2   Use the sauce immediately, or store in a screw-top jar in the refrigerator until needed.

- 56 calories
- 2.4 g saturated fat

ithai sauce

After years of tweaking, we have created a unique and delicious Thai sauce with the perfect balance of steeped flavors. It's something we are truly proud of, and its place as an itsu classic is now secure. Use it on potsus, as a dressing for steamed vegetables, or poured over white or brown rice. Stored in a screw-top jar, it will keep for up to a week in the refrigerator.

Serves 4

¼ cup coconut milk

1 teaspoon tomato paste

4–6 lime leaves, finely chopped

½ lemon grass stalk, finely chopped

¾-inch piece of fresh ginger root, grated

1 garlic clove, grated or crushed

1 shallot, finely chopped

2 teaspoons ground cumin

2 teaspoons lemon juice

1 teaspoon Thai fish sauce

1 teaspoon soy sauce

1 teaspoon dried red pepper flakes or ½ hot red Thai chile, chopped

1 teaspoon sugar or sugar alternative

1 teaspoon tamarind paste

1 teaspoon cornstarch

½ teaspoon salt

⅔ cup water

1 tablespoon cilantro leaves, chopped

1   Put all the ingredients, except the water and cilantro leaves, into a blender and blend to a smooth sauce. Alternatively, chop the ingredients as finely as possible by hand and combine in a bowl.

2   Put the sauce into a small saucepan and add the water. Slowly bring to a boil, stirring, then reduce the heat to a simmer and cook for 5 minutes.

3   Use the sauce immediately, adding the cilantro to serve, or store in a screw-top jar in the refrigerator until needed.

DESSERTS } & DRINKS }

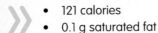

- 121 calories
- 0.1 g saturated fat

Hawaii five-fruit
This is our favorite fruit salad mix. If covered, it will keep in the refrigerator for several hours; alternatively, put it in a plastic container as a portable healthy snack or for a great picnic dessert.

Serves 4

½ medium mango, about 5 oz

½ medium melon, about 10½ oz

½ pineapple, about 10½ oz

1 cup blueberries

1 cup pomegranate seeds

zest and juice of ½ lemon

zest and juice of ½ lime

1 tablespoon honey, or any sugar alternative

1   Peel the mango, melon, and pineapple, and discard the melon seeds. Cut the flesh into bite-size pieces and mix in a bowl with the blueberries and pomegranate seeds.

2   Combine the lemon and lime juice in a small bowl, then add the honey and stir until dissolved.

3   Pour the honey mixture over the fruit and stir to combine.

Nutritional tip: Brightly colored fruits are loaded with antioxidants. Pomegranates and blueberries are said to help regulate blood pressure.

- 221 calories
- 5.4 g saturated fat

White chocolate yogurt & fruits

A rich, delicious dessert, this tastes decadent but is still butterfly light. Covered in nutritious fruit, it's a proper healthy treat.

Serves 2

2 oz white chocolate, broken into small pieces, or white chocolate drops

1 cup low-fat plain yogurt

1 teaspoon vanilla extract

1 cup mixture of fresh blueberries, raspberries, and blackberries, or whatever berries you desire

1   Put the chocolate into a heatproof bowl and melt in the microwave for 1 minute on High. Alternatively, sit the bowl over a small saucepan of simmering water (it must not actually touch the water) and warm over medium heat until melted.

2   Mix the yogurt with the vanilla extract and slowly add this mixture to the melted chocolate, mixing well to get a smooth consistency.

3   To serve, spoon the yogurt mixture into cups or bowls and sprinkle the berries on top.

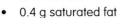

- 278 calories
- 0.4 g saturated fat

Baked bananas with no-dairy custard

Baking hot, sweet bananas coated in a creamy, caramel sauce made with dairy-free soft tofu. What could be more tempting?

Serves 2

2 very ripe bananas, unpeeled ....

zest and juice of ½ orange

1 tablespoon brown sugar or sugar alternative

½ cup soft/silken tofu

¼ cup sugar or sugar alternative

Nutritional tip: Bananas are full of potassium, vitamin B, and magnesium —all essential for good health.

1   Preheat the oven to 425°F.

2   Slice the bananas in half lengthwise and place them in a small baking dish. Sprinkle the orange zest, juice, and 1 tablespoon of brown sugar over them. Bake for 20 minutes.

3   Meanwhile, put the tofu into a bowl and whisk to a smooth paste.

4   Put the ¼ cup of sugar in a saucepan with 2 tablespoons water, bring to a boil, and continue boiling until it starts to turn brown and caramelize. Pour into the tofu and whisk well to combine.

5   Serve the bananas hot, with the caramel tofu alongside for pouring over them.

- 232 calories
- 8.3 g saturated fat

Classic chocolate mousse Find some

sweet little serving dishes or cups for the perfect portion size—small is beautiful when it comes to rich desserts. A hint of ginger gives these mini treats a subtle kick.

Serves 4

3½ oz good-quality bittersweet chocolate, broken into small pieces

2 teaspoons mirin

1 tablespoon light corn syrup

6 free-range eggs

3¼-inch piece of fresh ginger root, grated (about ⅓ cup)

1 Put the chocolate, mirin, and syrup into a heatproof bowl and melt in the microwave for 1 minute on High. Alternatively, sit the bowl over a small saucepan of simmering water (it must not actually touch the water) and warm over medium heat until melted.

2 Meanwhile, separate the eggs, putting the whites into a clean, grease-free bowl and the yolks into another. Set aside.

3 Place a strainer over the bowl of egg yolks. Hold the grated ginger in your hand over the strainer and squeeze the juice from it (you should get about a teaspoonful). Stir the juice into the yolks along with a tablespoon of water.

4 When the chocolate has melted, pour it slowly into the yolk mixture, stirring constantly until smooth.

5 Whisk the egg whites until they form soft peaks—try not to overwhisk them, or the mousse will become too stiff. When they are ready, gently but thoroughly fold them into the chocolate mixture so they are completely combined.

6 Pour the mousse into small cups, ramekins, or shallow serving dishes and place in the freezer for 20 minutes to chill or transfer to the refrigerator if not eating it immediately.

Nutritional tip: Good-quality dark chocolate contains anthocyanidins, which help regulate blood flow, and is also a good source of magnesium, which boosts energy levels.

- 168 calories
- 1.9 g saturated fat

Mixed berry frozen yogurt At itsu, we

use superhealthy pomegranate, blueberries, and strawberries in our frozen yogurt because they're packed with all the vitamins you need for a healthy life. Why not make double quantities and freeze the rest to enjoy another day?

Serves 2

2 tablespoons honey, or any sugar alternative

¾ cup plain yogurt (any type you like)

1½ cups mixed frozen berries ....

1 Chill 2 small bowls in the freezer.

2 Put the honey and yogurt into a blender and blend together. Add the berries and blend again.

3 Spoon the mixture into the chilled bowls and serve immediately.

Variation: Use any frozen fruit you desire; just remember to freeze it in small pieces so that it blends easily.

Nutritional tip: As well as being a good source of vitamin C, berries are rich in anthocyanins, which help maintain firm skin and flexible arteries, and they're good for your memory, too.

- 99 calories
- 1.7 g saturated fat

Green tea iced smoothie Blend up

this refreshing, energy-boosting smoothie in the morning for breakfast, or pour it into a thermos and enjoy as a low-calorie snack to perk you up during the day. It uses matcha, a powder made from ground green tea leaves.

Serves 2

a handful of ice cubes

¾ cup plain yogurt (any type you like) ....

1 tablespoon honey, or any sugar alternative

1 teaspoon matcha

1 Put all the ingredients into a blender and blend together until creamy and smooth.

2 Pour into tall glasses and serve while it's still ice cold.

Nutritional tip: Yogurt is full of bone-building calcium, while green tea is famed for its antioxidant properties, and is thought to protect against heart disease, too.

DESSERTS & DRINKS

- 148 calories
- no saturated fat

Pomegranate, pineapple & mint salad with lime syrup

Pomegranate seeds not only look and taste delicious, but they contain many powerful antioxidants. Here, they are paired with sweet pineapple and refreshing mint to make a simple yet delicious salad.

Serves 2

½ pineapple, about 10½ oz

seeds from ½ pomegranate (about ½–⅔ cup)

a few mint leaves

2½ tablespoons sugar or sugar alternative

2 tablespoons water

juice and zest of 1 lime

1 Cut the skin off the pineapple and cut the flesh into small pieces. Transfer to a small bowl and sprinkle with the pomegranate seeds and mint leaves.

2 Put the sugar and water into a small saucepan and bring to a boil. Continue boiling for 2 minutes to form a syrup. Remove from the heat and add the lime juice and zest.

3 Pour the hot syrup over the fruit and eat immediately, or cover and keep cool until required.

- 270 calories
- 2.1 g saturated fat

Quick watermelon & lime sorbet

Here's a really easy sorbet. If you freeze the watermelon in the morning, you can make it that night and enjoy it as a skinny dessert treat.

Serves 4

½ small watermelon (about 1½ lb)

3 tablespoons sugar or sugar alternative

¼ cup lime juice

1 Peel the watermelon and cut the flesh into small chunks (you can leave the seeds in). Place in a bowl and freeze overnight, or for at least 4 hours.

2 Put the frozen watermelon into a large blender, add the sugar and lime juice, and blend to a smooth sorbet. Serve immediately.

Nutritional tip: Watermelon contains the same antioxidants that are found in tomatoes. They contribute toward a healthy heart and are great to eat in the sun because they offer some natural UV protection.

- 56 calories
- no saturated fat

Detox zinger juice You don't need a

juicer to make this superhealthy juice, which has a special blend of
spices to help detox your body. It keeps for three days in the refrigerator.

Serves 4

⅔ cup beet juice (available from most supermarkets) ....

1⅔ cups apple juice

juice of ½ lemon

pinch of ground cloves

¼ teaspoon ground cinnamon

¼ teaspoon ground turmeric

1 cup water

Nutritional tip: Beet is believed to lower blood pressure and help repair muscles after exercise, while turmeric has anti-inflammatory properties.

1   Put all the ingredients in a lidded container and shake well.

2   Serve chilled, or bottle and carry with you as a portable health kick.

- 51 calories
- no saturated fat

Ginger & melon zinger Blend up this delicious

mixture in a blender for a healthy breakfast juice. If you want to store some, it will
keep, in a sealed container, for up to two days in the refrigerator.

Serves 4

2 cups melon pieces (any type)

1¼ cups apple juice

¾-inch piece of fresh ginger root, grated (about 2 tablespoons) ....

juice of 1 lime

⅔ cup water

1   Put all the ingredients into a blender and blend until smooth. Chill until needed, or serve with ice cubes for an instant, refreshing drink.

Nutritional tip: Ginger is anti-inflammatory—a great stomach soother.

- 20 calories
- no saturated fat

Iced i-tea
A refreshing beverage for a hot summer's day, this drink is based on green tea and is great for boosting the metabolism.

Serves 4

4 green tea bags

1½-inch piece of fresh ginger root, sliced

4–6 sprigs of mint

1 tablespoon honey, or any sugar alternative

juice of 1 lemon

3⅓ cups boiling water

2 handfuls of ice cubes

TO SERVE

ice cubes

lemon slices

mint leaves

1   Put the tea bags, ginger, mint, honey, and lemon juice into a large bowl, add the boiling water, and steep for 5 minutes.

2   Remove just the tea bags, then add the ice cubes. Chill in the refrigerator or freezer until needed.

3   Before serving, strain the liquid into a clean pitcher and serve with ice cubes, lemon slices, and mint leaves.

Left: Iced i-tea
Right: Ginger & melon zinger
Back: Detox zinger juice

Suppliers

All the ingredients in the recipes in this book are easy to find. Many are available from major supermarkets, and more specialty ingredients can be found easily online or in good Japanese or Asian food stores. Some excellent online sources are listed below. Listed, too, are some Japanese and Asian food suppliers that we recommend, and a few great fish suppliers of sashimi-grade fish as well as Japanese groceries.

GOOD ONLINE SOURCES

Amazon
This large online supplier has a gourmet food section that sells a large variety of ethnic and organic products sourced from different suppliers.
www.amazon.com

igourmet
Supplier of a huge variety of ingredients from around the world, including Japanese products such as Japanese rice, dried mushrooms, ponzu, nori, tamari sauce, pickled ginger, wasabi paste, and even yuzu mayonnaise. Look in their regional cuisine section of their Web site under "Japanese."
www.igourmet.com

Japan Super
Online supplier for a large range of authentic Japanese groceries, including gourmet and specialty foods, selling fresh, frozen, and dry goods as well as sashimi or sushi-quality fish.
japansuper.com

Kalustyan's
A New York City base supplier of fine specialty foods, Kalustyan's offers more than 4,000 varieties of spices, herbs, sweets, coffee, tea, and health snacks, imported from all over the world. Look for dried bonito flakes in their fish and seafood section. They also sell cellophane and soba noodles, various dried mushrooms, dried chiles, and jaggery.
kalustyans.com

Marukai eStore
Specializes in shipping Japanese products throughout the United States, including sashimi-quality seafood, as well as fresh vegetables, frozen produce, and dried products.
www.marukaiestore.com

Thai supermarket online
A supplier of Thai products, including fresh produce such as lemon grass and Thai chiles, canned exotic vegetables, pastes, sauces, and noodle and rice products.
www.importfood.com

World Spice Merchants
Supplier of a variety of spices and teas from around the world, they are an online source for wasabi.
www.worldspice.com

FOOD STORES

Mitsuwa Marketplace
Japanese supermarket chain with stores in several states, selling a range of Japanese products. Online shopping is also available on their Website.
www.mitsuwa.com

Trader Joe's
A chain of specialty grocery stores that sells gourmet, organic, and vegetarian foods, including its own brand name Japanese food labeled as Trader Joe-San. See their Website for store locations.
www.traderjoes.com

Whole Foods Market
Supplier of natural and organic foods, with more than 340 stores across North America and in the UK. See their Website for store locations.
www.wholefoodsmarket.com

Index